APOCALYPTIC
TERROR
AND MILLENNIAL
GLORY

APOCALYPTIC

TERROR

AND MILLENNIAL

GLORY

ROSS MCCALLUM JONES

Print information available on the last page.

Rev. date: 02/26/2020

To order additional copies of this book, contact:
Xlibris
1-800-455-039
www.Xlibris.com.au
Orders@Xlibris.com.au
777625

Contents

Commentary on Revelation

Appendices

Dedication

This book is gratefully dedicated to the Boo (Boko) church in Benin Republic, West Africa, with whom I lived and worked for much of my life. They taught me their language and culture and together we translated the Bible into their language and witnessed the conversion of thousands of Boo people in over forty towns and villages. Together we rejoice in the forgiveness and peace and courage and hope that come from knowing our Lord and Savior, Jesus the Messiah.

Abbreviations

Old Testament	**OT**	**New Testament**	**NT**
Genesis	Gen	Matthew	Matt
Exodus	Exod	Romans	Rom
Leviticus	Lev	1 Corinthians	1 Cor
Numbers	Num	2 Corinthians	2 Cor
Deuteronomy	Deut	Galatians	Gal
1 Samuel	1 Sam	Ephesians	Eph
Psalms	Ps	Philippians	Phil
Isaiah	Isa	Colossians	Col
Jeremiah	Jer	1 Thessalonians	1 Thess
Ezekiel	Ezek	2 Thessalonians	2 Thess
Daniel	Dan	1 Timothy	1 Tim
Hosea	Hos	2 Timothy	2 Tim
Zephaniah	Zeph	Hebrews	Heb
Haggai	Hag	1 Peter	1 Pet
Zechariah	Zech	2 Peter	2 Pet
Malachi	Mal	Revelation	Rev

Introduction

This commentary on the book of Revelation, otherwise known as the Apocalypse, is clear and simple, devotional and enlightening. Simple, because it is mainly concerned with the meaning of the text, and not so much with the author, date and background details many commentaries give. What I believe to be the correct interpretation is presented with minimal discussion of alternative interpretations. It is devotional in that it lays emphasis on the Bible text and what should be our basic response, not so much on exhortation or application to the Christian life. The general format for each passage is scriptures on the left-hand page and commentary on the right.

We are blessed if we read the words of this prophecy and take to heart what is written in them, because the time is near (Rev 1:3). Don't ignore reading the scripture portions carefully. Revelation is "apocalypse" in Greek and means "unveiling", an unveiling or revealing of what must soon take place before the end of the world as we know it. It was written by John, generally believed to be John, the son of Zebedee, one of Jesus' disciples in the first century. It is saturated with thoughts expressed by the Old Testament prophets concerning the end-times and the messianic kingdom. Below each passage of Revelation on the left-hand page are relevant verses from the Old Testament, of which words in italics are alluded to directly by John. Jesus confirmed the words of the prophets and we'll do well to study them and pay attention to them as to a lamp shining in a dark place (2 Pet 1:19).

More is revealed in the book of Revelation about the end of this age than what the prophets knew. Jesus himself is the revealer (Rev 1:1), and he reveals more to us here than what we have in the Gospels or the epistles. Even so, we are not told everything. There are many mysteries, and scholars have different interpretations. There is a lot of symbolism and use of metaphor in Revelation. The reader should not interpret these symbols and metaphors literally. It was revealed to John in a series of visions, so Revelation is like a picture book or a series of video clips. We need to think about the symbols and metaphors, and by using our imagination, picture it, and discern the truth being taught. This doesn't make it any less real. The symbols will be explained. Metaphors, by definition, should always be taken imaginatively, rather than literally. When John says he saw Jesus standing among seven golden lampstands with seven stars in his right hand, he is telling us what he saw in a vision. We are then told that the lampstands are seven churches, and the stars are the messengers of those churches. The primary meaning of "angel" in Greek is messenger. Imagine the picture; Jesus standing among gatherings of believers, whose job is to bear light to the world. He is there to protect, guide and empower the messengers, the church leaders, who through their preaching, teach the truth and inspire the believers.

The series of seals, trumpets and bowls all end with the Day of the Lord. There are many parallels between them. Some visions take place in heaven, others are on the earth. The climax of the book is the return of the Messiah and his millennial reign on earth. The purpose of the book is to inform the saints about the future events, so that they will be prepared for the terrible time of persecution, and to invite everyone to accept the free gift of salvation.

Part 1

CHAPTERS 1–5

THAT WHICH IS NOW

The Title and Origin of the Book

(Rev 1:1–3 ISV)

> This is the revelation of Jesus the Messiah, which God gave him to show his servants the things that must happen soon. He made it known by sending his messenger to his servant John, who testified about this message from God and the testimony about Jesus the Messiah. How blessed is the one who reads aloud and those who hear the words of this prophecy and obey what is written in it, for the time is near!
>
> **Dan 2:29** (NIV) As Your Majesty was lying there, your mind turned to things to come, and the revealer of mysteries showed you what is going to happen.
>
> **Rev 22:6** (NIV) The Lord, the God who inspires the prophets, sent his angel to show his servants the things that must soon take place.

This book is a revelation given by Jesus the Messiah. It is also about him, and it is given through the mediation of an angel to the apostle John. It is to be believed because it originates with God and it is the testimony of Jesus. It deals with the final catastrophic period of world history, when the Messiah, after mortal combat with the powers of evil, will emerge victorious.

John sees a series of visions, mostly prophecies about the future, relating to the end of this age and culminating in the end of the world. They describe the events which will precede the second coming of Jesus Christ, who is coming to rule the world. That is our hope. That is what we are looking forward to, and the reason why we pray: "May your kingdom come, may your will be done on earth."

God's servants (Greek = slaves) are God-fearing Christians who have surrendered their lives into his care. The time is near! It is hard to understand why something that was written nearly two-thousand years ago should be described as *near*. It seems that God wants us to keep these events in mind, and to live in expectation of the Messiah's return. His coming is our blessed hope, resulting in our salvation, including our resurrection and our glorification. This book is an especial encouragement to believers in time of persecution.

When John says, "the time is near", it is not a mistake; the concept is stated many times in the book. Jesus repeats the statement "I am coming soon" four times, and twice we have the phrase "what must happen soon". Greek-English lexicons sometimes give an alternative meaning for the Greek word ταχὺ, "soon", as "without unnecessary delay". The book of Revelation makes it clear that God has a plan; the timetable is set. Jesus will be revealed at the appointed time. Because these things are spoken of as taking place soon, some people assume the events of the book of Revelation are now in the past; they are now history. Some say the book was written before AD 70, so that they can include the destruction of Jerusalem as prophecy. However, everything leads up to the return of Jesus as Messiah, and that hasn't happened yet!

As the message was revealed to John in visions, the book is quite different to the historical books or the epistles. It is presented to us in picture form by means of symbols and metaphors to *show* us what must take place. But we must use our sanctified imaginations. There is a blessing for you here, if you hear the Apocalypse read or read it yourself, and more to the point, if you submit yourself to God and do his will.

GREETINGS TO CHURCHES AND PRAISE TO JESUS

(REV 1:4–6 ISV)

From John to the seven churches in Asia. May grace and peace be yours from the one who is, who was, and who is coming, from the seven spirits who are in front of his throne, and from Jesus the Messiah, the witness, the faithful one, the firstborn from the dead, and the ruler over the kings of the earth. To the one who loves us and has freed us from our sins by his blood and has made us a kingdom, priests for his God and Father, be glory and power forever and ever! Amen.

Exod 3:14 (NIV) *I AM WHO I AM.*

Exod 19:5–6 (NIV) Out of all nations you will be my treasured possession. … You will be for me a kingdom of priests and a holy nation.

Ps 89:27, 37 (NIV) I will appoint him [David] to be my firstborn, the most exalted of the kings of the earth. … It [David's line] will be established forever like the moon, the faithful witness in the sky.

Isa 55:4 (NIV) I have made him a witness to the peoples.

John greets the seven churches to whom this letter (the whole book) is addressed. The churches were in Asia Minor, modern-day Turkey, not far from the island of Patmos, where John was imprisoned. The benediction is from the eternal, triune God. "He who is, and who was, and who is to come" is a paraphrase of the divine name, YHWH, meaning I AM. "The seven spirits before the throne" refers to the Holy Spirit. And Jesus Christ is God the Son. Seven is a sacred number which is used fifty-five times in Revelation.

Jesus is the faithful witness. He came into the world to testify to the truth (John 18:37), the firstborn from the dead (Col 1:18) and the ruler of the kings of the earth, the blessed and only Ruler, the King of kings and Lord of lords (1 Tim 6:15). The final expression confirms the prophecy that the Messiah would rule the world (Ps 89:27).

John ascribes glory and power to Jesus because Jesus loves us, and nobody can separate us from the love of Christ (Rom 8:35), and also because Jesus has freed us from our sins by his blood. We have been justified by his blood, and even more certainly, we will be saved from God's wrath through him (Rom 5:9). And the final reason for praise is because he made us to be a royal body priests to serve his God and Father (Exod 19:5–6).

The expression "kingdom of priests" was first attributed to Israel, and now is applied to believers in Jesus. The word "kingdom" has the primary meaning of kingship or royal power. It refers to those who possess the kingship: the monarchy, the Messiah's government. Jesus is the coming king, and the saints, his people, will reign with him. They will inherit the kingdom (Matt 5:5, James 2:5) and reign with him (2 Tim 2:12) on earth (Rev 5:10). They will serve God as priests, because they alone have access to God and can mediate between him and unbelievers. The monarchy is a fulfilment of Moses' civil law, and the priesthood a fulfilment of the ceremonial law. The phrases "God's servants" (Rev 1:1) and "the saints" (Rev 5:8) always refer to Christians in Revelation. They are the royal family; they are heirs of God and co-heirs with Christ (Rom 8:17). That is the climax up to which this book inevitably builds.

Jesus' Second Coming

(Rev 1:7–8 ISV)

> Look! He is coming in the clouds. Every eye will see him, even those who pierced him, and all the tribes of the earth will mourn because of him. So be it! Amen. "I am the Alpha and the Omega," declares the Lord God, "the one who is, who was, and who is coming, the Almighty."
>
> **Isa 40:5** (NIV) And the glory of the Lord will be revealed, and all people will see it together.
>
> **Dan 7:13** (NIV) In my vision at night I looked, and there before me was one like a son of man, coming with the clouds of heaven.
>
> **Zech 12:10** (NIV) And I will pour out on the house of David and the inhabitants of Jerusalem a spirit of grace and supplication. They will look on me, the one they have pierced, and they will mourn for him as one mourns for an only child.

A key to understanding an author's purpose is to understand his literary structure. With greetings dispensed with, John opens his drama with two dramatic statements. The first is the announcement that the Messiah is coming, and every eye will see him. Isaiah connects his coming with Jerusalem. All the ends of the earth will see the salvation of Israel's God (Isa 52:7–10). The second is a statement by the Messiah himself, declaring that he is the Almighty God who was and is and is to come (cf. Rev 22:11–13). "He is coming with the clouds" is from a messianic prophecy in Daniel 7:13–14, from which Jesus took the title "Son of Man". He will come physically with clouds of angels (Mark 8:38) to establish his eternal kingdom and all nations will serve him.

The chapters leading up to Jesus' dramatic return describe a terrible time of tribulation that will occur under the reign of the Antichrist, culminating in the battle of Armageddon, when the whole world rebels against God. It will be a time of great suffering, as on the one hand, the Antichrist brings war and persecutes God's people, and on the other, as God pours out his wrath on a defiant world, including the greatest earthquake that humanity has known. The face of the earth will be destroyed and covered in darkness. Telecommunications will be down, so the world's population won't see Jesus' return on phones or TV. His coming will be like lightning flashing across the whole sky.

John alludes to a prophecy in Zechariah 12:10–12 that predicts that the Jews will look on the one they have pierced, and all their clans will mourn for him. It is the Jews – "all the tribes of the land"– who will mourn for him as they are converted at this time. The unbelievers won't mourn for him; they will curse God because of the plagues (Rev 16:9, 11, 21). However, the glory and noise of Jesus' return will be so great that his return will be visible to all.

Alpha and Omega are the first and last letters of the Greek alphabet. The Messiah is the Lord God, the first and the last, the beginning and the end. He controls all human history. In Revelation, we find that Jesus, the Son of God, is often pictured seated on the throne together with the Father. Jesus said that he and the Father are one (John 10:30) and that the Father is in him and he is in the Father (John 10:38). Father and Son have equal authority throughout Revelation. Praise is given in one breath to him who sits upon the throne and to the Lamb (Rev 5:13. 7:10). The throne of God and of the Lamb will be in the city, and his servants will serve *him* (22:3). The pronoun "him" relates to both God and the Lamb, the Father and the Son.

John, the Writer

(Rev 1:9–11 ISV)

> I am John, your brother and partner in the oppression, kingdom, and patience that comes because of Jesus. I was on the island called Patmos because of the word of God and the testimony about Jesus. I came to be in the Spirit on the Day of the Lord, when I heard a loud voice behind me like a trumpet, saying, "Write on a scroll what you see, and send it to the seven churches: Ephesus, Smyrna, Pergamum, Thyatira, Sardis, Philadelphia, and Laodicea."

John never reveals his identity beyond "John", but early tradition is unanimous that the author was John the apostle. He identifies himself with fellow Christians. He is their brother and companion, patiently enduring and suffering with them, imprisoned on the isle of Patmos.

Paul said that we have the privilege, not only of believing in Christ, but also of suffering for him (Phil 1:29). He said that we are heirs of God and co-heirs with Christ, *if* we share in his sufferings. In this way we will share in his glory (Rom 8:17). This theme of martyrdom is emphasized in many verses (Rev 2:10, 3:10, 6:9–11, 12:17, 13:7, 10, 14:12–13, 16:6, 17:6, 18:24, 20:4). The church needs to be patient and endure, knowing that a kingdom awaits them. They will reign with the Messiah over the entire world. The kingdoms of this world will become the kingdom of the Messiah, and he will reign for ever and ever (Rev 11:15).

The Lord's day is Sunday, the first day of the week, the day the early Christians chose to meet for worship. John was 'in the Spirit' (cf. Rev 4:2), a state of spiritual awareness produced by the Holy Spirit, in which John saw his visions. Visions, in contrast to dreams, are seen while one is awake. He was instructed to write down what he saw in his visions on a scroll, a sheet of parchment, which in the first century was the equivalent of a book. What he saw included specific messages to the seven churches mentioned in verse 4, but in addition, it included all the visions that he saw in the entire book of Revelation.

John heard the voice of the Lord Jesus speaking to him and his voice sounded like a trumpet. When Moses received the ten commandments, he heard God speaking to him on Mount Sinai and his voice sounded like thunder (Exod 19:19).

The Son of Man

(Rev 1:12–16 ISV)

Then I turned to see who was talking to me, and when I turned I saw seven gold lamp stands. Among the lamp stands there was someone like the Son of Man. He was wearing a long robe with a gold sash around his chest. His head and his hair were white like wool, in fact, as white as snow. His eyes were like flames of fire, his feet were like glowing bronze refined in a furnace, and his voice was like the sound of raging waters. In his right hand he held seven stars, and out of his mouth came a sharp, two-edged sword. His face was like the sun when it shines with full force.

Dan 7:9, **13** (NIV) The Ancient of Days took his seat. His clothing was as white as snow; the hair of his head was white like wool. ... in my vision at night I looked, and there before me was *one like a son of man*, coming with the clouds of heaven.

Dan 10:5–6 (NIV) I looked up and there before me was a man dressed in linen, with a belt of fine gold from Uphaz around his waist. His body was like topaz, his face like lightning, his eyes like flaming torches, his arms and legs like the gleam of burnished bronze, and his voice like the sound of a multitude.

Ezek 1:26–27 (NIV) Above the vault over their heads was what looked like a throne of lapus lazuli, and high above on the throne was a figure like that of a man ... from his waist up he looked like glowing metal, as if full of fire, and from there down he looked like fire.

Ezek 43:2 (NIV) I saw the glory of the God of Israel coming from the east. His voice was like the roar of rushing waters, and the land was radiant with his glory.

John saw Jesus standing there with his face shining like the sun as it did at the transfiguration (Matt 17:2) symbolizing his glory. Coming out of his mouth was a sharp double-edged sword (Heb 4:12) symbolizing the power and authority of his word. In his hand were seven stars which represent the messengers of the churches. Some interpret them as guardian angels of the churches, but why would the Lord hold angels in his hand and address commendations and rebukes to them and tell them to repent? The primary meaning of the Greek word ἄγγελος is "messenger", but it is often used for angels. The church leader who brings God's messages to his flock is the most appropriate interpretation. The title of the book Malachi means "my messenger" and refers to the prophet Malachi. As in Greek, the Hebrew word means both messenger and angel.

There was a golden lampstand with seven lamps on it in the temple with which Jews were familiar. Instructions on its manufacture are given in Exodus 25:31–40. The significance of a lampstand and its lamps is of course that they give light. It is a fitting symbol for the local church.

The title "Son of Man" is used by Jesus to show himself to be the Messiah, as described in Daniel's prophecy (Dan 7:13). It is a title that expresses both divinity and humanity. In each context where it is used, it points to the Messiah's present lowliness or to his future glory. In the vision that Daniel saw, God gives glory and kingship to him who appears before him in human form, coming with the clouds of heaven, that all people and nations might honor him. The long robe with a golden sash around the chest was the high priest's attire. Jesus is our high priest, as well as being the coming King, and he makes us to be a kingdom of priests. This is a vision of the glorified Messiah, who was described in a similar way by Daniel, Isaiah, and Ezekiel, all of whom saw a glorified human Messiah in their visions.

The Resurrected and Glorified Jesus

(Rev 1:17–20 ISV)

When I saw him, I fell down at his feet like a dead man. But he placed his right hand on me and said, "Stop being afraid! I am the first and the last, the living one. I was dead—but look!—I am alive forever and ever! I have the keys of Death and Hades. Therefore, write down what you have seen, what is, and what is going to happen after this. The secret meaning of the seven stars that you saw in my right hand and the seven gold lamp stands is this: the seven stars are the messengers of the seven churches, and the seven lamp stands are the seven churches.

Isa 41:4b (NIV) I, the LORD – with the first of them and with the last – I am he.

Isa 44:6 (NIV) I am the first and I am the last; apart from me there is no God.

Mal 2:7 (NIV) For the lips of a priest ought to preserve knowledge, because he is the messenger of the LORD Almighty and people seek instruction from his mouth.

John collapses before this glorious apparition of Jesus, but Jesus reassures him that he is the risen Christ who holds the keys of death and Hades. As Paul said, Christ was raised from the dead and cannot die again; death no longer has mastery over him (Rom 6:9). Christ is alive forever and holds the keys of death and Hades, the place of departed spirits. It is he who has the power to raise the dead on the day of resurrection. Jesus gave the keys of the kingdom of heaven to Peter, so that he and the other apostles could preach the gospel and open the way for believers to enter his earthly kingdom and eternal life (Matt 16:19). Later he breathed on them and told them to receive the Holy Spirit. If they forgave anyone their sins, they would be forgiven; if they didn't forgive them, they wouldn't be forgiven (John 20:23–24). That baton has now passed to us.

The fact that Jesus holds the keys of death and Hades is a great encouragement to the saints; it inspires them in times of tribulation and persecution to persevere and be faithful to their Lord, even if it involves martyrdom. Jesus is the First and the Last; he is sovereign over the whole length of human history, and as he said in John's gospel, he is the resurrection and the life. Whoever believes in him will live, even if he dies (John 11:25). He died, and yet he is alive forevermore, and the same will be true for those who believe in him.

There is a three-fold division of the book; what is now (Rev 1–5), what is going to happen (Rev 6–18), and Messiah's return and reign (Rev 19–22). The whole purpose of God in creating the world is the salvation of those who believe in him, Christians, those who are organized into churches and are led by God's messengers.

Jesus stands among the seven churches and holds seven stars in his hand. The stars are God's messengers to the seven churches, and it is to them that the seven letters of chapters 2–3 are written, not to angels. The messenger is the church leader; an overseer or shepherd, the one responsible before God for his "flock". The Greek word "you" is always singular throughout these letters, but sometimes the whole church is addressed (Rev 2:24). At the end of each letter, all the faithful are requested to take note of what the Spirit was saying to the churches.

Ephesus – the Church that Lost Its First Love

(Rev 2:1–7 ISV)

To the messenger of the church in Ephesus, write: 'The one who holds the seven stars in his right hand, the one who walks among the seven gold lamp stands, says this: 'I know what you've been doing, your toil, and your endurance. I also know that you cannot tolerate evil people. You have tested those who call themselves apostles, but are not, and have found them to be false. You have endured and suffered because of my name, yet you have not grown weary. However, I have this against you: You have abandoned the love you had at first. Therefore, remember how far you have fallen. Repent and go back to what you were doing at first. If you don't, I will come to you and remove your lamp stand from its place—unless you repent. But this is to your credit: You hate the actions of the Nicolaitans, which I also hate. Let everyone listen to what the Spirit says to the churches. To everyone who conquers I will give the privilege of eating from the tree of life that is in God's paradise.'

Gen 2:9 (NIV) In the middle of the garden were the tree of life and the tree of the knowledge of good and evil.

Gen 3:22 (NIV) The man has now become like one of us, knowing good and evil. He must not be allowed to reach out his hand and take also from the tree of life and eat, and live forever.

Jer 2:2 (NIV) I remember the devotion of your youth, how as a bride you loved me.

Each letter begins with a different description of the author, Jesus, as he was described in chapter 1. Paul spent two years ministering to the church in Ephesus. He was preceded by Aquila and Priscila and followed by Timothy and John. So, the saints there had great teachers. There were no church buildings at that time, the word "church" refers to a group of believers who met weekly, usually on Sundays in someone's home.

The seven letters are addressed to the *messenger* of each church, and the commendations, complaints and corrections relate primarily to him, but "whoever has an ear" is encouraged to listen to what the Spirit says to the churches.

The Ephesian church leader had worked hard and persevered in the face of persecution. He had made a stand against false teachers and prophets and had not grown weary. The first love is the initial enthusiasm or devotion (Jer 2:2) the leader had when he first believed. That initial love had waned; his love for God, and maybe his love for others also. If a leader's love has grown cold, he has lost his purpose, and ceases to be a true leader. Loving God and your neighbor are the greatest of all the commandments. He may have been doctrinally correct, hating the practices of the Nicolatian heresy, but faith must always be accompanied by love. Jesus tells his servant to repent; otherwise his church would be moved to another location or allowed to die.

The tree of life gives immortality to those who eat it fruit. After Adam and Eve sinned in the garden of Eden, the tree of life was denied them. Paradise in Revelation is the New Jerusalem which God has prepared for us, wherein God and believers will be restored to perfect fellowship, and man will rule as he was originally created to do (Rev 22:2, 14, 19).

Smyrna – the Suffering Church

(Rev 2:8–11 ISV)

To the messenger of the church in Smyrna, write: 'The first and the last, who was dead and became alive, says this: 'I know your suffering and your poverty—though you are rich—and the slander committed by those who claim to be Jews but are not. They are the synagogue of Satan. Don't be afraid of what you are going to suffer. Look! The devil is going to throw some of you into prison so that you may be tested. For ten days you will undergo suffering. Be faithful until death, and I will give you the victor's crown of life. Let everyone listen to what the Spirit says to the churches. The one who conquers will never be hurt by the second death.

Dan 1:12 (NIV) Please test your servants for ten days.

God allows his servants to live in poverty and with afflictions, because they can be sorrowful, yet always rejoicing, poor, yet making many rich, having nothing, yet possessing everything (2 Cor 6:10). God chose those who are poor in the eyes of the world to be rich in faith, and to inherit the kingdom he promised those who love him (James 2:5). Despite their poverty, they are the fortunate ones; their sins are forgiven, they are children of God and co-heirs with Christ. To have Christ is to have everything.

Unfortunately, in different times and places, Christians are called upon to live in hostile environments, where they are treated as second-class citizens and suffer economically. The Smyrna leader suffered much. He had to put up with the slander of an actively hostile Jewish population, whose synagogue belonged to Satan rather than God.

Polycarp, a leader at Smyrna, was an early martyr. The devil is behind these persecutions, which are allowed to test the faith of God's servants for a sufficiently long time (ten days). Jesus encourages him to be faithful, even if it means death, because he will give him the crown of life; the reward of eternal life and ruling with the Messiah. Christians who persevere and stand firm to the end will be saved (Matt 10:22). The second death is hellfire, called the lake of fire (Rev 20:14), and the fiery lake of burning sulfur (Rev 21:8). It has no power over overcomers who will be resurrected, thereby becoming immortal.

Millions of Christians today live in hostile environments, because they belong to ethnic or religious minorities. Thousands die as Christian martyrs each year, especially the leaders. John tells us that there will be an enormous number of martyrs in the last days, so we need to think seriously about Jesus' command to be faithful, even to the point of death, knowing that he will give us the crown of life.

Pergamum – the Church that Tolerates False Teaching

(Rev 2:12–17 ISV)

To the messenger of the church in Pergamum, write: 'The one who holds the sharp, two-edged sword, says this: 'I know where you live. Satan's throne is there. Yet you hold on to my name and have not denied your faith in me, even in the days of Antipas, my faithful witness, who was killed in your presence, where Satan lives. But I have a few things against you: You have there some who hold to the teaching of Balaam, the one who taught Balak to put a stumbling block before the people of Israel so that they would eat food sacrificed to idols and practice immorality. You also have some who hold to the teaching of the Nicolaitans. So repent. If you don't, I will come to you quickly and wage war against them with the sword of my mouth. Let everyone listen to what the Spirit says to the churches. To the one who conquers I will give some of the hidden manna. I will also give him a white stone. On the white stone is written a new name that no one knows except the person who receives it.'

Exod 16:4, 31 (NIV) I will rain down bread from heaven for you … The people of Israel called the bread manna.

Num 31:16 (NIV) They were the ones who followed Balaam's advice and enticed the Israelites to be unfaithful to the Lord in the Peor incident, so that a plague struck the Lord's people.

Isa 56:5 (NIV) To them I will give within my temple and its walls a memorial and a name better than sons and daughters; I will give them an everlasting name that will endure forever.

John 6:32 (NIV) It is my Father who gives you the true bread from heaven.

Pergamum was the official center of emperor worship in Asia (present-day western Turkey), so it is described as a place where Satan lived and had his throne. Pergamum is known for its many martyrs. Satan and his demons are active in all our towns and cities, but like God, they live in a different realm. Satan influences governments to be anti-Christian, and demons enslave people through superstitions and animistic religion. Demon possession and black magic, involving invocation of evil spirits, are still common in many parts of the world. Balaam symbolizes false teachers who compromise with morality. This leader turned a blind eye toward some in his congregation who embraced this false teaching.

Satan is mentioned thirty-five times in the New Testament, including four times in these letters. We should not doubt his existence. He is sometimes called the dragon, or the ancient serpent (from Gen 3), or the devil. He is a deceiver and an accuser. Paul calls him the ruler of the domain of the air, the spirit who is presently at work in those who are disobedient (Eph 2:2) He says that our real struggle is not against humans, but against the cosmic powers of the darkness around us, the evil spiritual forces in the heavenly realm (Eph 6:12).

The sword in Jesus' mouth represents his authority (cf. Rev 19:15, 2 Thess 2:8), where the Lord Jesus overthrows the lawless one with the breath of his mouth. The promises of Jesus in each letter apply to the time when he returns, and the saints are resurrected. He is the resurrection and the life (John 11:25), the true bread from heaven (John 6:32). Whoever eats that hidden manna will live forever. The white stone was sent as an invitation. Here, it is an invitation to the messianic banquet, and the recipient will have a secret name. Jesus will also have a name on him, known only to himself (Rev 19:12).

THYATIRA – THE CHURCH THAT TOLERATES PAGANISM

(REV 2:18–25 ISV)

To the messenger of the church in Thyatira, write: The Son of God, whose eyes are like flaming fire and whose feet are like glowing bronze, says this: 'I know what you've been doing—your love, faithfulness, service, and endurance—and that your last actions are greater than the first. But I have this against you: You tolerate that woman Jezebel, who calls herself a prophet and who teaches and leads my servants to practice immorality and to eat food sacrificed to idols. I gave her time to repent, but she refused to repent of her immorality. Look! I am going to strike her with illness. Those who commit adultery with her will also suffer greatly, unless they repent from acting like her. I will strike her children dead. Then all the churches will know that I am the one who searches minds and hearts. I will reward each of you as your actions deserve. But as for the rest of you in Thyatira—you who do not hold to this teaching and who have not learned what some people call the deep things of Satan—I won't burden you with anything else. Just hold on to what you have until I come.'

1 Kings 21:25 (NIV) There was never anyone like Ahab, who sold himself to do evil in the eyes of the LORD, urged on by Jezebel his wife.

Jer 17:10 (NIV) I the Lord search the heart and examine the mind, to reward each person according to their conduct, according to what their deeds deserve.

After initial commendation for his faith, love, service and perseverance, the Lord blames the church leader for tolerating a so-called prophetess who led people into immorality and idolatry. Converts from pagan backgrounds often find it hard to change their worldview and relinquish their previous spiritual convictions, including idolatry and food laws. Jesus declared all foods clean (Mark 7:18–19) and good for Christians to eat, but Paul warned against eating food offered to idols. Those who fear and follow their own traditions about food ignore and nullify the word of God. Let the word of God go deep into our lives. Doctrine is important, because it determines our behavior. Both bad habits and bad beliefs must be repented of. Otherwise we can expect suffering in this world and the next (Rev 2:22).

Committing adultery with this prophetess means joining with her in her idolatrous ways and its associated immorality, including sacrificing to idols. She and her followers were to be punished with sickness and death. They would be made examples of, so that other believers would not be tempted to join them. The Son of God, whose eyes are like blazing fire, knows the hearts and minds of everyone, and at times repays them according to their behavior.

Tolerance is the buzzword of our day. Non-judgmentalism means that we have no right to judge the actions of others, no matter how immoral or sinful we believe them to be. There is no right or wrong, no male or female, no place for the ten commandments. The leader had tolerated Jezebel and her teachings, and some in the church had been led astray. Maybe they were taught that what was done in the body would not affect their spiritual lives. Or maybe they were taught that to appreciate the grace of God fully, they must first experience the depths of evil. But God says that we should be holy, because he is holy (1 Pet 1:16). Jesus encourages the faithful to persevere until he returns.

Overcomers will Rule
with the Messiah

(Rev 2:26–29 ISV)

> To the person who conquers and continues to do what I've commanded to the end, I will give authority over the nations. He will rule them with an iron scepter; shattering them like clay pots. Just as I have received authority from my Father, I will also give him the morning star. Let everyone listen to what the Spirit says to the churches.
>
> **Num 24:17** (NIV) A star will come out of Jacob; a scepter will rise out of Israel.
>
> **Ps 2:6–9** (NIV) I have installed my King on Zion, my holy mountain. I will proclaim the LORD's decree: He said to me, "You are my Son; today I have become your father. Ask me, and I will make the nations your inheritance, the ends of the earth your possession. You will break them with a rod of iron; you will dash them to pieces like pottery."

The messianic Psalm 2 is quoted here. Immediately after his return, the Messiah will rule over the nations. He will rule them with severity until all his enemies are subdued. He will restore the world that has been marred by the curse and will be nearly completely destroyed by man in the last days. As the Jewish Messiah, he will revive Israel's kingdom (Acts 1:6) and reign from Jerusalem.

The promise here to the overcomers is that they will rule with him. The authority that his Father has given him will be shared with the saints who will be resurrected or raptured and transformed at Jesus' return. They will reign with the Messiah in his kingdom. The word "kingdom" means kingship or royal authority. The saints are not the subjects of his kingdom, they are children of God; heirs of God, and co-heirs with Christ. They will take part in the Messiah's government, as illustrated in the parable about the coins. One good servant's reward for his faithfulness in doing small things was to have charge of ten cities in his master's coming kingdom (Luke 19:17).

The creation is waiting in eager expectation for the sons of God to be revealed (Rom 8:19). During the Messiah's 1000–year reign the creation will be liberated from its bondage to decay and brought into the glorious freedom of the children of God (Rom 8:21).

Jesus declares that he is the Root and Offspring of David, and the bright Morning Star (Rev 22:16). The morning star is the planet Venus that signals the dawn. Jesus' return is the dawn of a new age, the dawn of eternal life for the overcomers. That seems to be the meaning of the promise of the morning star. Daniel 12:3 says those who manifest wisdom will shine like the brightness of the expanse of heaven, and those who turn many to righteousness will shine like the stars forever and ever.

Sardis – the Dying Church

(Rev 3:1–6 ISV)

To the messenger of the church in Sardis, write: 'The one who has the seven spirits of God and the seven stars says this: 'I know what you've been doing. You are known for being alive, but you are dead. Be alert, and strengthen the things that are left, which are about to die. I note that your actions are incomplete before my God. So remember what you received and heard. Obey it, and repent. If you are not alert, I will come like a thief, and you won't know the time when I will come to you. But you have a few people in Sardis who have not soiled their clothes. They will walk with me in white clothes because they are worthy. The person who conquers in this way will wear white clothes, and I will never erase his name from the Book of Life. I will acknowledge his name in the presence of my Father and his angels. Let everyone listen to what the Spirit says to the churches.'

Exod 32:32 (NIV) But now, please forgive their sin – but if not, then blot me (Moses) out of the book you have written.

Ps 69:28 (NIV) May they be blotted out of the book of life and not be listed with the righteous.

Dan 12:1b (NIV) But at that time your people – everyone whose name is found written in the book – will be delivered.

Jesus holds the seven spirits of God. This phrase expresses the presence of the Holy Spirit whom he promised to send to his followers from the Father. The Holy Spirit is our Counselor, the Spirit of Truth (John

15:26). Jesus is presently seated at the right hand of God and he continues to send the Spirit to believers, just as he did on the day of Pentecost (Acts 2:33). We have already seen that the seven stars in his hand are the seven messengers of the seven churches. The churches are under his supervision.

Only those who have the Spirit of Christ living in them belong to Christ. It is they who are spiritually alive and who will be resurrected (Rom 8:9–11). Those without the Spirit of God are fake Christians; they are described as asleep or dead; they don't know God. The church leader at Sardis was asleep. He is told to wake up, repent, and obey the word of God that he had heard. Otherwise Jesus will return when he doesn't expect him, and he will be like one of the foolish virgins who were not prepared when the bridegroom returned (Matt 25:10–13).

However, there were some in the Sardis assembly who were not asleep. They were spiritually alive, and their sins had been forgiven. They had received the righteousness that comes from God, symbolized by the white robes. They were worthy, because their faith and their conduct had proved them to be worthy. They will be the overcomers on that day when Christ returns. Their names are written in the Lamb's book of life and will never be erased. Christ will vouch for them before the Father (Matt 10:32). They are not nominal Christians; they are genuine. Jesus told his disciples to rejoice because their names are recorded in heaven (Luke 10:20).

Philadelphia – the Evangelistic Church

(Rev 3:7–10 ISV)

To the messenger of the church in Philadelphia, write: 'The one who is holy, who is true, who has the key of David, who opens a door that no one can shut, and who shuts a door that no one can open, says this: 'I know what you've been doing. Look! I have put in front of you an open door that no one can shut. You have only a little strength, but you have obeyed my word and have not denied my name. I will make those who belong to the synagogue of Satan—those who claim to be Jews and aren't, but are lying—come and bow down at your feet. Then they will realize that I have loved you. Because you have obeyed my command to endure, I will keep you from the hour of testing that is coming to the whole world to test those living on the earth.'

Isa 22:22 (NIV) I will place on his shoulder the key to the house of David; what he opens no one can shut, and what he shuts no one can open.

Isa 60:14 (NIV) The children of your oppressors will come bowing before you; all who despise you will bow down at your feet and will call you the City of the LORD, Zion of the Holy One of Israel.

Dan 12:1 (NIV) There will be a time of distress such as has not happened from the beginning of nations until then. But at that time your people – everyone whose name is found written in the book – will be delivered.

Christ holds the key of David. As king, he controls access to the house of David, the royal household and during this present church age, people of faith are being called out of all nations. They are the children of God and during the messianic reign it is they who will constitute the royal household and reign with Christ.

After Paul's first missionary journey, he returned to Antioch and reported all that God had done through them and how he *had opened the door of faith to the Gentiles* (Acts 14:27). The Philadelphian leader was an evangelist, he was busy spreading the gospel. He didn't have much strength, but Christ knew his deeds and he placed before him an open door. The Lord has been opening doors for his servants for centuries, and people have heard the gospel and responded. They have entered the kingdom as members of the royal house of David. God opens doors for us so we can serve him (1 Cor 16:9, 2 Cor 2:12, Col 4:3).

This leader had a major conflict with a synagogue who opposed him. During the messianic reign, every knee will bow to Jesus, and all those who oppressed Christian workers will then be forced to acknowledge that they are the beloved of the Messiah.

The reward for his endurance and faithfulness is that he and other faithful people alive at the time will be kept from the hour of trial that is coming upon the whole world. This is not a promise of pretribulation rapture as taught by some, and which has little scriptural support, but rather a promise of preservation through trial in accordance with Jesus' prayer to the Father, when he said he was not asking God to take them out of the world, but that he would protect them from the evil one (John 17:15). In the history of the spread of Christianity, there have always been martyrs. The Lord does not necessarily save his people from persecution and martyrdom. We are called not only to believe in Jesus, but also to suffer for him (Phil 1:29). The souls of those who had been slain for the word of God were told to wait until the number of their fellow servants and brothers who were to be killed as they had been was completed (Rev 6:11).

An hour of trial may refer to any persecution of Christians, but here the hour of trial that is going to come upon the whole world is the Great Tribulation (Mark 13:19), which occurs at the end of this age. This trial is the focus of Revelation 6 – 18. During this time an out-of-control dictator will cause havoc and God's wrath will be poured out on unbelievers. It is not directed toward believers, but the destruction will be so universal, that Christians will be affected. When Jesus said that not a hair of our heads will perish (Luke 21:18), he was talking about our eternal security, not our physical safety. As the martyrs will soon be resurrected, nothing perishes.

The Philadelphian leader wouldn't be around for the Great Tribulation, but the warnings and promises to these church leaders applies to churches and Christians of any age.

It is obvious from the following chapters that Christians will suffer persecution during the last days, but they are not the objects of God's wrath. By persevering and remaining faithful unto death, they will not love their lives when faced with death (Rev 12:11) and their greatest victory will be achieved. Christians who believe in a pretribulation rapture save themselves from the Great Tribulation and then replace themselves with converts from that period. It doesn't make sense. Once the church is raptured, the door is shut, entry into the Messiah's monarchy is closed. Those who are alive at the Lord's coming will be raptured at his coming, and at that same time God will bring with Jesus those who have fallen asleep (died) in him. The Second Coming, the Resurrection, and the Rapture are all one event (1 Thess 4:15-17).

OVERCOMERS WILL BE PILLARS IN GOD'S TEMPLE

(REV 3:11–13 ISV)

I am coming soon! Hold on to what you have so that no one takes your victor's crown. I will make the one who conquers to become a pillar in the sanctuary of my God, and he will never go out of it again. I will write on him the name of my God, the name of the city of my God (the new Jerusalem coming down out of heaven from God), and my own new name. Let everyone listen to what the Spirit says to the churches.

Ezek 48:35b (NIV) And the name of the city from that time on will be: THE LORD IS THERE.

A pillar is stable and permanent. The righteous will not be literal pillars, but they are indwelt by the Spirit of God and will dwell permanently with God. Paul said that we are God's temple because God's Spirit lives in us (1 Cor 3:16). In Christ we are being built together to become a dwelling in which God lives by his Spirit (Eph 2:22).

The 144,000 have the name of the Lamb and the Father written on their foreheads (Rev 14:1); a sure sign of possession. Here Jesus writes his own name and the Father's name and the name of New Jerusalem on the overcomers, and also his new name. They have a special relationship to Jesus and the Father, and New Jerusalem will be their eternal home. The throne of God and of the Lamb will be in the New Jerusalem, and we will serve him. We will see his face and his name will be on our foreheads (Rev 22:3–4). New Jerusalem is the bride of Christ, the glorified church. It is a metaphor for the universal community of God's people. The saints are God's royal family, and they will rule with him

29

for ever and ever. Only those whose names are written in the Lamb's book of life may enter this city (community). This is our destiny on (or above) the new earth. The city will come down out of heaven from God. The dwelling of God will be with men. He will live with them, and they will be his people, and he'll be their God (Rev 21:3).

All the promises made to the overcomers relate to our eternal union with God as described in Revelation 21:1 – 22:5: The promises are: a home in the New Jerusalem (21:2), no second death (21:8), names written in the book of life (21:27), access to the tree of life (22:2), reigning forever (22:5), a new name (22:4), they belong to God, and the morning star (2:28) a promise of entry into eternity.

LAODICEA – THE LUKEWARM CHURCH

(REV 3:14–22 ISV)

To the messenger of the church in Laodicea, write: 'The Amen, the witness who is faithful and true, the originator of God's creation, says this: 'I know your actions, that you are neither cold nor hot. I wish you were cold or hot. Since you are lukewarm and neither hot nor cold, I am going to spit you out of my mouth. You say, "I am rich. I have become wealthy. I don't need anything." Yet you don't realize that you are miserable, pitiful, poor, blind, and naked. Therefore, I advise you to buy from me gold purified in fire so you may be rich, white clothes to wear so your shameful nakedness won't show, and ointment to put on your eyes so you may see. I correct and discipline those whom I love, so be serious and repent! Look! I am standing at the door and knocking. If anyone listens to my voice and opens the door, I will come in to him and eat with him, and he will eat with me. To the one who conquers I will give a place to sit with me on my throne, just as I have conquered and have sat down with my Father on his throne. Let everyone listen to what the Spirit says to the churches.'

God does not like lukewarm Christians. He is a jealous God, meaning that he demands exclusive service (Deut 6:14–15). "Amen" signifies that which is valid and binding or changeless. Christ is the truth (John 14:6), he is trustworthy and faithful, in contrast to the Laodicean leader. He is the ruler of God's creation. The word "ruler" can also mean that Jesus is the origin or first cause of creation. He is not the beginning of creation; that would mean he was the first thing created.

The Laodicean church was rich, but wealth is not the strength of a church or its leader. Maybe he had not invested in God, but in this world. His focus was not on the spiritual but on the physical and material. Wealth without the gospel results in spiritual poverty and blindness. His state before God was pitiful and wretched. And he was naked, because he was not clothed with the righteousness that Christ provides.

He is counselled to buy gold refined in the fire (genuine riches of faith – 1 Pet 1:7), white clothes (righteousness provided by God (Matt 6:33), and eye-salve to correct his spiritual blindness. Paul prayed that the hearts of the Ephesian Christians might be enlightened so that they might know the glorious inheritance that God has called them to (Eph 1:18–19). The Lord wants his servants to have true wealth, not the passing riches of this world.

As all good fathers should do, the Lord rebukes and disciplines those whom he loves. He is standing at the door and knocking, and the invitation is addressed to individuals rather than churches. This picture was made famous by Holman Hunt's painting "The Light of the World", where Christ is knocking at a door overgrown with vines, and there is no doorknob on the outside. Those who open the door to him and receive him and believe on his name become children of God (John 1:12). To the contrary, anyone who does not have the Spirit of Christ does not belong to him (Rom 8:9). He promises to come in, if only we will open the door.

The overcomers, those who are saved by trusting in Jesus and persevering through trial, have a glorious future. They are called according to God's purpose. They are predestined to be conformed to the likeness of his Son. They are justified and glorified. This glorification consists of being resurrected with immortal bodies and reigning with Christ for a thousand years on this earth and on into eternity. Jesus will give them the right to sit with him on his throne (on earth), just as Jesus sat down with his Father on his throne (in heaven).

Christ is knocking and waiting for individuals to invite him in. He is doing it now. It has nothing to do with his return. He wants to come in and eat with us; to have fellowship with us, sharing spiritual food in an atmosphere of intimacy, affection and companionship. This is real life. He who has an ear, let him hear what the Spirit says to the churches.

John's Vision of God's Throne

(Rev 4:1–3 ISV)

After these things, I saw a door standing open in heaven. The first voice that I had heard speaking to me like a trumpet said, "Come up here, and I will show you what must happen after this." Instantly I was in the Spirit, and I saw a throne in heaven with a person seated on the throne. The person sitting there looked like jasper and carnelian, and there was a rainbow around the throne that looked like an emerald.

Gen 9:16 (NIV) Whenever the rainbow appears in the clouds, I will see it and remember the everlasting covenant between God and all living creatures of every kind on the earth.

Isa 6:1 (NIV) *I* [Isaiah] saw the Lord, high and exalted, seated on a throne, and the train of his robe filled the temple.

Ezek 1:26–28a (NIV) Above the vault over their heads was what looked like a throne of lapus lazuli, and high above on the throne was a figure like that of a man. I [Ezekiel] saw that from what appeared to be his waist up he looked like glowing metal, as if full of fire; and that from there down he looked like fire; and brilliant light surrounded him. Like the appearance of a *rainbow* in the clouds on a rainy day, so was the radiance around him.

Dan 7:9 (NIV) As I looked, thrones were set in place, and the Ancient of Day took his seat. His clothing was as white as snow, the hair of his head was white like wool. His throne was flaming with fire, and its wheels were all ablaze.

John, in a vision, sees an open door in heaven. Then Jesus calls him to come and see what must soon take place. He enters heaven through the door, as in a dream, and what he sees, he records in the rest of the book. He is fully conscious, and he sees into the future. He is not really in heaven, and what he sees is not reality, it is a vision. All the same, what he sees is accurately reflecting the things that must take place, the visions recorded in chapters 4–22.

In his vision, he sees God sitting on his throne. Can you imagine God sitting on a chair? The vision expresses God's sovereignty. His glory resembles the glory of precious stones, and a green rainbow surrounds the throne. Imagine the brilliant color. Unfortunately, we don't know exactly what jasper and carnelian looked like, but this is metaphor; fuel for our imagination. Daniel says his throne was flaming with fire, and its wheels were all ablaze. Ezekiel's vision of the Lord was a figure like that of a man; not meaning that God is a man, but man's body is the most perfect body that we know of, the most appropriate body for rendering visible God's invisible spiritual being. Attributing a human form or personality to God is called an anthropomorphism.

Since the days of Noah, the rainbow has been the sign of God's covenant with mankind; God's commitment that he would never again destroy living things by a worldwide flood. God is always faithful to the covenants he makes.

John does not tell us what the person on the throne looks like, but our impression will be that in visions at least, he looks like a man. So, he is pictured as sitting on a throne, wearing clothes, and having a head of white hair. We know that man was created in the image of God, but we can't be certain how this relates to God's spiritual form. However, in the future we will see his face (Rev 22:4).

God's Heavenly Council

(Rev 4:4–7 ISV)

Around the throne were 24 other thrones, and on these thrones sat 24 elders wearing white robes and gold victor's crowns on their heads. Flashes of lightning, noises, and peals of thunder came from the throne. Burning in front of the throne were seven flaming torches, which are the seven spirits of God. In front of the throne was something like a sea of glass as clear as crystal. In the center of the throne and on each side of the throne were four living creatures full of eyes in front and in back. The first living creature was like a lion, the second living creature was like an ox, the third living creature had a face like a human, and the fourth living creature was like a flying eagle.

Ezek 1:4–6, 10, 22 (NIV) I looked, and I saw a windstorm coming out of the north – an immense cloud with flashing lightning and surrounded by brilliant light. The center of the fire looked like glowing metal, and in the fire was what looked like four living creatures. In appearance their form was human, but each of them had four faces and four wings. [10]Their faces looked like this: Each of the four had a face like a human being, and on the right side each had the face of a lion, and on the left the face of an ox; each also had the face of an eagle. [22]Spread out above the heads of the living creatures was what looked something like a vault, sparkling like crystal, and awesome.

Ezek 10:12 (NIV) Their entire bodies, including their backs, their hands and their wings, were completely full of eyes, as were their four wheels.

Who are these twenty-four rulers surrounding God's throne? The Greek word πρεσβύτερος, from which "priest" is derived, means elder, official, or leader. It was used both for members of the Jewish Sanhedrin and for leaders of the churches. The white clothing is symbolic of their imputed righteousness, and the golden crowns of their being royalty. Other crowns described in the epistles are crowns of righteousness, life and glory. The number twenty-four represents the twelve Jewish tribes from the old covenant, and the twelve apostles from the new covenant. Their names are written on the gates and foundations of New Jerusalem (Rev 21:12, 14). The saints are co-heirs with Christ, so it is not surprising to see them connected with God's throne. Man was created to rule the world, and only redeemed man is given this privilege. So, these twenty-four elders represent the saints, the church.

Thunder and lightning express the awesomeness of God's majesty and power. The seven lamps represent the Holy Spirit, who is never represented in scripture as reigning or on the throne, despite his deity. The glassy sea is immortalized in the hymn "Holy, holy, holy", by the line "all the saints adore thee, casting down their golden crowns around the *glassy sea.*" The sea of glass is a sea that is as transparent as glass, and as clear as crystal. It symbolizes the tranquility of God's throne. Imagine the colors of the throne being reflected in it. A throne room is at the center of government, and here, everything is under control. The sea of glass contrasts with the turbulent seas of the world.

The four living creatures, also called cherubim, are throne attendants who represent the created order, which will be liberated from its bondage to decay during the Messiah's reign on earth. So, it is appropriate that these creatures join in praising God. The lion, ox, man and eagle represent wild animals, domestic animals, mankind and birds. The fact that they are in heaven gives us hope that God's creation will in some way continue to exist throughout eternity.

Worshiping God in Heaven

(Rev 4:8–11 ISV)

Each of the four living creatures had six wings and were full of eyes inside and out. Without stopping day or night they were saying, "Holy, holy, holy is the Lord God Almighty, who was, who is, and who is coming." Whenever the living creatures give glory, honor, and thanks to the one who sits on the throne, who lives forever and ever, the 24 elders bow down and worship in front of the one who sits on the throne, the one who lives forever and ever. They throw their victor's crowns in front of the throne and say, "You are worthy, our Lord and God, to receive glory, honor, and power, because you created all things; they came into existence and were created because of your will.

Isa 6:2–3 (NIV) Above him were seraphs, each with six wings: With two wings they covered their faces, with two they covered their feet, and with two they were flying. And they were calling to one another: "Holy, holy, holy is the LORD Almighty; the whole earth is full of his glory."

In Ezekiel the cherubim have four wings, and in Isaiah the seraphs have six wings as here. They represent creation, just as the twenty-four elders represent redeemed humanity, but they also portray God's attributes as reflected in creation: his majesty (lion), his omniscience (eagle), his omnipotence (ox), and his personhood (man). They are throne attendants, covered with eyes, front and back and under the wings, indicating that nothing escapes their attention. In Genesis 3:24, cherubim were stationed at the entrance to the Garden of Eden to guard the way to the tree of life. They praise and thank the sovereign, eternal God day and night, acknowledging his majesty.

The twenty-four elders bow down and join in the worship, acknowledging his sovereignty by casting their crowns down before him. They rule with God but are completely submissive to him. They praise him as Creator of all things and recognize that his will is supreme. He does whatever he wants and is the source of all life. The key word is "holy" which relates to his deity, his perfection, his apartness, his authority and power.

This is the throne room in heaven. This is the center of the universe, where God controls and sustains everything. This is the place where man's destiny is determined. Human history is under God's control, and the next chapter introduces us to the Lamb, the Savior of the world, who will reveal to John, and to us, the events which must occur before the end of this age. The Lamb is the one who was sacrificed, so that people from every tribe and language and people and nation might be redeemed. He is also the coming Messiah, who will come to defeat the enemy and eliminate all evil. He will rule the world and restore it to its pre-curse condition, and then hand his kingdom over to God the Father.

The Scroll of the World's Destiny

(Rev 5:1–4 ISV)

> Then I saw in the right hand of the one who sits on the throne a scroll written on the inside and on the outside, sealed with seven seals. I also saw a powerful angel proclaiming with a loud voice, "Who is worthy to open the scroll and break its seals?" No one in heaven, on earth, or under the earth could open the scroll or look inside it. I began to cry bitterly because no one was found worthy to open the scroll or look inside it.
>
> **Ps 139:16** (NIV) All the days ordained for me were written in your book before one of them came to be.
>
> **Dan 12:1b, 4, 9** (NIV) But at that time your people – everyone whose name is found written in the book – will be delivered. … But you, Daniel, roll up and seal the words of the scroll until the time of the end. Many will go here and there to increase knowledge. …. Go your way, Daniel, because the words are rolled up and sealed until the time of the end.
>
> **Ezek 2:9–10** (NIV) Then I looked, and I saw a hand stretched out to me. In it was a scroll, which he unrolled before me. On both sides of it were written words of lament, mourning and woe.

The scroll is a book which was written before creation and on which are recorded all the details of our lives (Ps 139:16), and the entire history of the world. It rests in the hand of God who knows and controls everything. Daniel was told things that were written in this 'Book of Truth' (Dan 10:21), and that at a certain time everyone whose name was written in the book would be delivered (Dan 12:1).

The books of the Bible and other documents used to be written on scrolls. They could be rolled up and sealed with wax, and then stamped for security. So, Daniel was told to shut up (in archives) and seal (preserve for posterity) what had been revealed to him from that book. Copies were made, which were made public.

This scroll is of unparalleled significance. In it is written the destiny of the world as determined by the sovereign will of God. We live in the last days, the time that extends from Pentecost to the Second Coming. It is time for what God has determined to be revealed. But we are not given dates, or names of people and places; prophecy is necessarily obscure.

As the seals are removed, some things are revealed. The destiny of the world is a broad subject, but more specifically, it is Jesus the Messiah who is revealed, and not only he. Paul tells us that the creation is waiting in eager expectation for the sons of God to be revealed (Rom 8:19). If Jesus' return to earth as the King of kings is one climax to the book, an associated climax is the glorification of the children of God, and another is the liberation of creation from its bondage to decay. Paul considers that our present sufferings are not worth comparing with the glory that will be revealed in us (Rom 8:18).

Most of the book of Revelation describes the sufferings that we might experience before our glorification. Jesus said that nations will continue to be at war with each other, and there will be famines and earthquakes, but these are only the beginning of birth pains (Matt 24:7–8). As the seals are broken, the events of the last days are revealed to John in a series of visions, and through John to the servants of God who read his book. Jesus told his disciples about this renewal of all things, which will occur when he sits on his glorious throne and his disciples reign with him (Matt 19:28). But who is worthy to bring history to its foreordained consummation and reveal the future rulers? A mighty angel made proclamation everywhere, and John was very upset that no one worthy was found.

The Messiah Is Worthy to Open the Scroll

(Rev 5:5–8 ISV)

"Stop crying," one of the elders told me. "Look! The Lion from the tribe of Judah, the Root of David, has conquered. He can open the scroll and its seven seals." Then I saw a lamb standing in the middle of the throne, the four living creatures, and the elders. He looked like he had been slaughtered. He had seven horns and seven eyes, which are the seven spirits of God sent into all the earth. He went and took the scroll from the right hand of the one who sits on the throne. When the lamb had taken the scroll, the four living creatures and the twenty-four elders bowed down in front of him. Each held a harp and a gold bowl full of incense, the prayers of the saints.

Gen 49:9–10 (NIV) You are a lion's cub, Judah. ... The scepter will not depart from Judah, nor the ruler's staff from beneath his feet, until he to whom it belongs shall come, and the obedience of the nations shall be his.

Ps 141:2 (NIV) May my prayer be set before you like incense.

Isa 11:10 (NIV) In that day the Root of Jesse [David's father] will stand as a banner for the peoples; the nations will rally to him, and his resting place will be glorious.

Isa 53:7 (NIV) He was oppressed and afflicted, yet he did not open his mouth; he was led like a lamb to the slaughter, and as a sheep before its shearers is silent, so he did not open his mouth.

One of the elders tells John not to weep. Someone has been found worthy! He is the Lion of the tribe of Judah, the promised Messiah, the coming king of Israel. He has triumphed. Jesus conquered sin and Satan and death by his self-sacrifice on the cross. He now has the authority to defeat all his enemies, both human and demonic, to establish his kingdom on earth, and to bring this earth to a fitting conclusion. Because of Jesus, history will have a good ending, like a fairy tale. Life is not meaningless.

Jesus descended from the tribe of Judah, the tribe from which kings arose. He is the conquering Messiah to whom the scepter belongs (Gen 49:10). But rather than him being depicted as a lion, he is seen as a sacrificial animal, a lamb that looks as if it has been slain, bearing the marks of slaughter. Imagine our Savior in his humiliation, how he suffered and died for us. But now he has ascended to heaven and is standing in the center of the throne, elsewhere described as seated at the right hand of the Father. His exalted position means equality with God. His seven horns depict his universal power, and his seven eyes are identified here as the seven spirits of God sent out into all the earth; the Holy Spirit, whom he sends on a worldwide mission, to regenerate and to indwell believers (John 16:7), and to mark them as a seal (Eph 4:30), until Christ returns to establish his kingdom.

Jesus comes and takes the scroll from the hand of the Father while all who are present fall down prostrate to worship him. They hold harps, symbolizing the musical accompaniment, and bowls of incense, symbolizing the constant prayer of the saints, as in the Lord's prayer, that his kingdom will come, and that his will might be done on earth as it is in heaven. The prayers of the saints of all ages have been heard, and now God will answer them. These prayers play an essential part in bringing justice to the earth, and judgment upon the rebellious inhabitants.

Praising the Messiah who Suffered

(Rev 5:9–14 ISV)

They sang a new song: "You are worthy to take the scroll and open its seals, because you were slaughtered. With your blood you purchased people for God from every tribe, language, people, and nation. You made them a kingdom and priests for our God, and they will reign on the earth." Then I looked, and I heard the voices of many angels, the living creatures, and the elders surrounding the throne. They numbered 10,000's times 10,000 and thousands times thousands. They sang with a loud voice, "Worthy is the lamb who was slaughtered to receive power, wealth, wisdom, strength, honor, glory, and praise!" I heard every creature in heaven, on earth, under the earth, and on the sea, and everything that is in them, saying, "To the one who sits on the throne and to the lamb be praise, honor, glory, and power forever and ever!" Then the four living creatures said, "Amen!", and the elders bowed down and worshipped.

Ps 40:3a (NIV) He put a new song in my mouth, a hymn of praise to our God.

Dan 7:10b (NIV) Thousands upon thousands attended him, ten thousand times ten thousand stood before him.

The Lamb is worthy to open the seals and reveal the future, because by his death he paid the price for the salvation of millions of souls; people from all language groups. He is the one who will bring the world to its planned consummation. He gave his life as a ransom for many (Matt

20:28). They were bought with a price (1 Cor 6:20), with the precious blood of Christ, a lamb without blemish or defect (1 Pet 1:19).

The saints have been made a kingdom of priests to serve their God, as was explained in 1:6. The added information here is that they will reign *on earth*. However, some translate *over the earth*, which I prefer, because after the resurrection, our home will be in the New Jerusalem, not on earth. We will rule over the earth with Christ for a thousand years from a different space-time dimension, and then forever and ever (Rev 22:5). This is eternal life! This is what we were saved for! This is our glorification.

Millions of angels will join in this celebration in heaven. God's will will be accomplished. The Lord Jesus Christ will receive power, wealth, wisdom, strength, honor, glory and praise. Angels will not be exalted like the saints will be, when they are glorified and reign with Christ (Heb 2:5–8). The angels are not seated on thrones, and they don't address the Lamb directly. They are described as ministering spirits sent to serve those who will inherit salvation (Heb 1:14). All creation joins in to praise both Father and Son. The living creatures say, "Amen", while the elders, who represent the saints, fall down and worship.

The living creatures and the elders sing a new song because of new circumstances. They celebrate a new act of divine deliverance. Not only are the saints saved from their sins and made righteous, they will rule the nations on earth under their king, the Messiah, and all of creation will be liberated from its bondage to decay.

Part 2

CHAPTERS 6 – 18

THAT WHICH WILL TAKE PLACE LATER

A Horseman Goes Forth
to Conquer

(Rev 6:1–2 ISV)

> Then I saw the lamb open the first of the seven seals. I heard one of the four living creatures say with a voice like thunder, "Go!" Then I looked, and there was a white horse! Its rider had a bow, and a victor's crown had been given to him. He went out as a conqueror to conquer.
>
> **Ezek 39:3 (NIV)** Then I will strike your bow from your left hand and make your arrows drop from your right hand.
>
> **Zech 6:1–5** (NIV) I looked up again, and there before me were four chariots coming out from between two mountains – mountains of bronze. The first chariot had red horses, the second black, the third white, and the fourth dappled – all of them powerful. I asked the angel who was speaking to me, "What are these, my lord?" The angel answered me, "These are the four spirits of heaven, going out from standing in the presence of the Lord of the whole world."

The imagery of the four horsemen of the apocalypse comes from the prophet Zechariah, where they are portrayed with chariots. All the latter Jewish prophets made predictions about the last days and the messianic kingdom, especially Isaiah and Zechariah. The four chariots with their different colored horses (Zech 6:1–8) represent four destructive forces (winds), sent out from God into the world. They are agents of divine judgment sent to punish the nations who have oppressed God's people. Behind the mysteries and judgments of life on earth, the eternal, omnipotent, omniscient God is at work, but a closer look exposes evil rulers, false messiahs, and evil spiritual forces as the real cause of the problems. The four horses are personifications of war, bloodshed, famine and death.

In Revelation 6:8 the four horsemen are described as having been given power over a fourth of the earth to kill by sword, famine and plague, and by the wild beasts of the earth. They are to bring about the death of one fourth of mankind. Each time the Lamb opens a seal, one of the living creatures says, "come", a command for the horse and its rider to come. The living creatures, who represent the living creation, are initiating the divine commands from the throne.

Some interpret the rider of the white horse as the Antichrist. Others see him as Christ, who goes out into the whole world to proclaim the gospel and save people from every nation, tribe, people and language. He said that the gospel must first be preached to every nation (Mark 13:10). In this case the white horse is identified with the white horse of Revelation 19:11. Christ is building his church, but he doesn't go himself; he sends his servants out to do the work. And he is never associated with a bow. The four horsemen fit better together, as agents of divine judgment. The first horseman represents a victorious warrior or dictator.

A comparison can be made between the horsemen and the preliminary signs of the end of the age that Jesus gave (Matt 24, Mark 13, Luke 21), which included false Messiahs (white), wars (red), earthquakes and famines (black). Jesus said that these are only the beginning of birth pains. Revelation 6–18 consists of visions about the Great Tribulation which will occur during the seven years preceding the return of the Messiah.

Two Horsemen Bring
War and Famine

(Rev 6:3–6 ISV)

> When the lamb opened the second seal, I heard the second
> living creature say, "Go!" A second horse went out. It was fiery
> red, and its rider was given permission to take peace away from
> the earth and to make people slaughter one another. So he was
> given a large sword. When the lamb opened the third seal, I
> heard the third living creature say, "Go!" I looked, and there
> was a black horse! Its rider held a scale in his hand. I heard
> what sounded like a voice from among the four living creatures,
> saying, "One day's ration of wheat for a day's wage, or three day's
> ration of barley for a day's wage! But don't damage the olive oil
> or the wine!"

The color of the horses does not exactly match the four horses of
Zechariah 6, but they have the same significance. The white horse
represents conquest, the red horse bloodshed, the black horse famine,
and the pale horse death. The word "pale" describes a yellowish green
color, which is used to describe a sick or dead person. They represent
destructive forces, and they will affect everyone on earth, not just
unbelievers.

Wars have been constant throughout the ages at different times and
different places. Jesus said that when we hear about wars or rumors of
wars, we should not be alarmed. That will happen, but it's not the end.
There will be wars and earthquakes and famines in different places, but
that is just the beginning (Mark 13:7–8). The four horsemen symbolize
these sufferings, but more especially under the rule of the Antichrist,
the last great dictator.

The pair of scales represents famine, which results in inflated prices for basic foodstuffs. The price of grain is ten to twelve times the normal. Famine often follows wars and earthquakes. If the sufferings are due to war and what follows war, man is responsible. If it is from an act of God, then God is responsible. To understand these severe judgments, we need to take note of Paul's words in Romans 1:18–20, where he said that God will express his anger against man's godlessness and wickedness, because in their wickedness. they suppress the truth about him and his creation. God's eternal power and divine nature can be clearly seen in all that he has been made, so atheists have no excuse.

The destiny of the world won't be disclosed until all the seals are opened, all the trumpets are blown, and all the bowls of God's wrath are poured out.

A Fourth Horseman Brings Death to a Quarter of the World's Population

(Rev 6:7–8 ISV)

> When the lamb opened the fourth seal, I heard the voice of the fourth living creature say, "Go!" I looked, and there was a pale green horse! Its rider's name was Death, and Hades followed him. They were given authority over one-fourth of the earth to kill people using wars, famines, plagues, and the wild animals of the earth.
>
> **Ezek 5:17** (NIV) I will send famine and wild *beasts* against you, and they will leave you childless. Plague and bloodshed will sweep through you, and I will bring the sword against you. I the LORD have spoken.

The pale horse is a personification of death and Hades, Hades being the underworld, the place of the dead. They will kill a quarter of the world's population by warfare, famine, plague and wild beasts. We need to ask ourselves how and why a quarter of the world's population should be killed in this way. Not only that; in chapter 9 after the sixth trumpet is blown, a third of mankind is said to be killed, while in chapter 16 after the blowing of the seventh trumpet all the cities of the world collapse. Imagine all those skyscrapers and multi-story residential buildings collapsing and the carnage that would produce.

The first horseman *was given* a crown; God permits conquerors and dictators. The second and fourth horsemen *were given* power to kill, again by God's permission. We will inevitably ask ourselves why God is portrayed as wanting to kill one quarter of mankind, billions of people. God knows everything and he is a God of love, so his decisions can be trusted. In Isaiah 13:12, God said he would make man scarcer than pure gold. In the context of the need of persistence, Jesus asked if he would find faith on earth when he returns (Luke 18:8).

We naturally love God's kindness, but we don't like to talk much about his severity. Paul said we should consider both the kindness and severity of God (Rom 11:22). Part of the divine character may seem to us to be severe, hard or harsh. It is the opposite of his goodness, kindness or grace. God is kind to those who take refuge in him, and he is severe with those who reject him. This is the wrath of God which makes his deity manifest in merited punishment. God is just, and according to justice, evil must be punished. God didn't make people wicked; he made them capable of wickedness; and they have decided for it, and they will be punished. At the end of the world we find this punishment more specifically directed to unbelievers, even before judgment day. The Day of the Lord is actually a part of the final judgment. That is why the text says that authority was given to death and Hades to kill a quarter of the world's population. Because of God's sovereignty, the scriptures see God as the cause behind all events. What he allows, he wills.

In 2 Peter 3:9 we read that the Lord is being patient with us; he doesn't want anyone to perish; he wants everyone to come to repentance.

MARTYRS FOR JESUS

(REV 6:9–11 ISV)

When the lamb opened the fifth seal, I saw under the altar the souls of those who had been slaughtered because of the word of God and the testimony they had given. They cried out in a loud voice, "Holy and true Sovereign, how long will it be before you judge and take revenge on those living on the earth who shed our blood?" Each of them was given a white robe. They were told to rest a little longer until the number of their fellow servants and their brothers was completed, who would be killed as they themselves had been.

Deut 32:43 (NIV) Rejoice, you nations, with his people, for he will avenge the blood of his servants; he will take vengeance on his enemies and make atonement for his land and people.

Ps 119:84 (NIV) How long must your servant wait? When will you punish my persecutors?

The four apocalyptic horsemen have ridden forth portraying the troubled times that precede the consummation of this present age. When Jesus opens the fifth seal, John sees a vision of Christian martyrs. Every year of every century there have been faithful Christians sacrificing their lives for their Lord. Worldwide, these Christian martyrs number in the tens of thousands each year. According to a leading human rights watchdog, Open Doors USA, 100 percent of Christians in twenty-one countries around the world experience persecution for their faith in Christ and over 215 million Christians faced high levels of persecution in 2016. Most of these countries are in the Middle East, but it also happens in North Korea, Vietnam, India, Kenya and Nigeria.

John saw the martyrs under the altar. This doesn't mean they had bodies; it is a vision. In the Mosaic sacrificial rituals, the blood of the slaughtered animals was poured out at the base of the altar. It is a way of saying that their premature deaths on earth are from God's perspective a sacrifice on the altar of heaven, because the life of a creature is in the blood (Lev 17:11).

It is a part of every Christian's calling to be prepared for martyrdom. Jesus said, if anyone wants to follow him, he must deny himself and take up his cross and then follow. If you are intent on hanging on to your life, you will lose it. If you are prepared to lose your life for Jesus sake, you will save it (Matt 10:38–39). The martyrs were slaughtered because of the word of God and the testimony they had maintained. In other words, because they were Christians who believed in the Bible.

They were crying out to God to take vengeance on "the inhabitants of the earth", which in Revelation always refers to mankind in its hostility to God. White robes are for believers who through faith have washed their robes and made them white in the blood of the Lamb (Rev 7:14). They are usually referred to as the saints (holy ones), or God's servants. They are to wait until the day when their number will be complete, the day when Jesus will return to earth as victorious king, the day when God's people will be resurrected.

The martyrdom of the saints is also regarded as a judgment. Peter said, if we suffer as Christians, we should not be ashamed, but praise God that we bear his name. For it is time for judgment to begin with the family of God (1 Pet 4:16–17). Persecutions and martyrdom are divinely sent judgments intended to purify and perfect God's people.

The Day of the Lord

(Rev 6:12–14 ISV)

Then I saw the lamb open the sixth seal. There was a powerful earthquake. The sun turned as black as sackcloth made of hair, and the full moon turned as red as blood. The stars in the sky fell to the earth like a fig tree drops its fruit when it is shaken by a strong wind. The sky vanished like a scroll being rolled up, and every mountain and island was moved from its place.

Isa 34:4 (NIV) All the stars of the heavens will be dissolved and the sky rolled up like a scroll; all the starry host will fall like withered leaves from the vine, like shriveled figs from the fig tree.

Ezek 38:19–20 (NIV) In my zeal and fiery wrath I declare that at that time there shall be a great earthquake in the land of Israel. The fish of the sea, the birds in the air, the beasts of the field, every creature that moves along the ground, and all the people on the face of the earth will tremble at my presence. The mountains will be overturned, the cliffs will crumble, and every wall will fall to the ground.

Zech 14:4 (NIV) On that day his feet will stand on the Mount of Olives, east of Jerusalem, and the Mount of Olives will be split in two from east to west, forming a great valley, with half of the mountain moving north and half moving south.

With the opening of the seventh seal (8:1), there is silence in heaven for half an hour, because God's wrath has been poured out, the world has been judged, and the destruction is beyond belief. The opening of the sixth seal describes the Day of the Lord, which is the day when the Messiah returns. The day of judgment has come and the face of planet earth has been changed forever. Mountains and islands are gone, every wall has fallen down, the cities of the world are destroyed. The Lord has punished mankind for its evil and made them scarcer than pure gold. Ezekiel prophesied a great earthquake which would cause everyone on the face of the earth to tremble and mountains to be overturned. This can be equated with Zechariah prophesied that the Messiah would come and stand on the Mount of Olives and it would split in two (Zech 14:4). The unbelievers flee from the splendor of his majesty and tremble at his presence. Zechariah continues, "And so the LORD my God will come, and all his holy ones will be accompanying you" (Zech 14:6d ISV). The holy ones are the saints who have just been resurrected.

So, the opening of the sixth seal reveals the turbulent events that accompany the Lord's return. Events associated with the seventh trumpet and the seventh bowls of God's wrath help us interpret what this cosmic disturbance is all about, but here the focus is on the physical disturbances. After the seventh trumpet is blown, loud voices in heaven give thanks because the kingdom of the world has become the kingdom of our Lord and his Messiah and he has begun to reign. The nations raged, but his wrath has come (Rev 11:15–18).

After the seventh bowl is poured out there is a great earthquake, the greatest the world has ever known (Rev 16:18), which causes the cities of the world to collapse (Rev 16:19). The sun and moon are obscured by smoke, the stars no longer shine. John's vision shows us how people will actually see things in the sky; the heavenly bodies themselves will not be affected. The stars won't fall to earth, although there may be meteors, or great boulders dropping down to earth from volcanos. Imagine the loss of life when cities collapse with the resulting fires. The day when Jesus returns will be a day of darkness and total chaos, but for the church it is will mean resurrection and glorification.

World Leaders Cower
before the Messiah

(Rev 6:15–17 ISV)

Then the kings of the earth, the important people, the generals, the rich, the powerful, and all the slaves and free people concealed themselves in caves and among the rocks in the mountains. They told the mountains and rocks, "Fall on us and hide us from the face of the one who sits on the throne and from the wrath of the lamb. For the great day of their wrath has come, and who is able to endure it?"

Ps 76:7 (NIV) *Who can stand* before you when you are angry?

Isa 2:19 (NIV) People will flee to caves in the rocks and to holes in the ground from the fearful presence of the LORD and the splendor of his majesty, when he rises to shake the earth.

Hos 10:8b (NIV) Then they will say to the mountains, "Cover us!" and to the hills, "Fall on us!".

Zeph 1:14–15 (NIV) The great day of the LORD is near – near and coming quickly. The cry on the day of the LORD is bitter; the Mighty Warrior shouts his battle cry. That day will be a day of wrath – a day of distress and anguish, a day of trouble and ruin, a day of darkness and gloom, a day of clouds and blackness.

Mal 3:2 (NIV) But who can endure the day of his coming? Who can stand when he appears?

The Day of the Lord is a single day, because it is the day the Lord returns to earth in power and glory with all his angels. The mighty earthquake will only need a few minutes to wreak havoc upon the world, but the devastation will be complete. The armies that surround Jerusalem will be in complete disarray as they try and hide from the majestic Messiah. Only the Lord's people will endure the day of his coming; no one else will withstand it. But Jesus' coming will be the climax. Who can stand when he appears?

After the opening of the sixth seal John sees the reaction of the world population to these chaotic events and the coming of the Messiah. Influential people can usually manage to escape from disasters, but not from this one. Kings and princes, political and military leaders, all the rich and mighty will try and hide from God on that day, to save themselves from the wrath of the Lamb, who has now arrived as king. They will look for anywhere to hide. They will even ask the mountains and hills and rocks to fall on them. Such will be their terror before the splendor of the Lord. Only the saints will stand tall on that day.

Jesus has opened six of the seven seals, and they do not reveal a pretty picture, but rather judgment on a sinful world. A similar picture will be painted as the seven trumpets are blown and the seven bowls of God's wrath are poured out. The seals, the trumpets and the bowls are all in their own way describing the darkness and gloom of the Great Tribulation, and they all end with a description of the Lord's return. It is the climax of the battle between God and Satan, between good and evil, between the rulers of the earth and the servants of God.

144,000 Israelis Sealed

(Rev 7:1–8 ISV)

After this, I saw four angels standing at the four corners of the earth. They were holding back the four winds of the earth so that no wind could blow on the land, on the sea, or on any tree. I saw another angel coming from the east having the seal of the living God. He cried out in a loud voice to the four angels who had been permitted to harm the land and sea, "Don't harm the land, the sea, or the trees until we have marked the servants of our God with a seal on their foreheads." I heard the number of those who were sealed: 144,000. Those who were sealed were from every tribe of Israel: 12,000 from the tribe of Judah were sealed, 12,000 from the tribe of Reuben, 12,000 from the tribe of Gad, 12,000 from the tribe of Asher, 12,000 from the tribe of Naphtali, 12,000 from the tribe of Manasseh, 12,000 from the tribe of Simeon, 12,000 from the tribe of Levi, 12,000 from the tribe of Issachar, 12,000 from the tribe of Zebulun, 12,000 from the tribe of Joseph, and 12,000 from the tribe of Benjamin were sealed.

Isa 11:12 (NIV) He will raise a banner for the nations and gather the exiles of Israel; he will assemble the scattered people of Judah from the four quarters of the earth.

Jer 49:36 (NIV) I will bring against Elam _the four winds_ from the four quarters of heaven.

Ezek 9:4 (NIV) Go throughout the city of Jerusalem and put a mark on the foreheads of those who grieve and lament over all detestable things that are done in it.

The sixth seal brought us to the very end of this present age, when the Messiah will come. This chapter goes back a little in time, but still within the final years. It concerns God's servants whose souls John saw under the altar when the fifth seal was opened. The word "servants" occurs ten times in Revelation. Twice it refers to the prophets, everywhere else it refers to believers in general (Rev 1:1). The four angels are restraining destructive forces that will come from all directions. These "four winds of the earth" are the same as the "four winds of heaven" that Zechariah spoke of (Rev 6:5), but these are a final and more destructive manifestation. In anticipation of the judgments which will affect the earth, sea and trees following the blowing of the first two trumpets in chapter 8, God protects his servants, not by removing them from the earth, but by sealing them (Eph 1:13–14), marking them as the possession of the Lamb and the Father (Rev 14:1, 22:5). The destructive forces that are restrained by the angels are conquest, war, famine and death. When released, these, probably nuclear, forces will destroy land, sea and vegetation. The trumpet judgments add rivers and springs and heavenly bodies to the list of affected areas.

The number sealed is 144,000. It is symbolic (12 x 12 x 1000) and should not be taken literally. There will be more than 144,000 saints on earth. They are sealed with the seal of the *living* God, who intervenes on behalf of his people. We are told that they come from all the tribes of Israel, twelve thousand from each of the twelve tribes. Most interpret them as the "Israel of God", a symbolic term that Paul used to refer to all of God's people (Gal 6:16).

Judah is mentioned first because royalty comes from this tribe. Joseph's sons, Manasseh and Ephraim, became tribes, but Joseph is listed here as well, so Dan is omitted. Some interpreters see the 144,000 as the living servants of God who survive on earth, while the great multitude (Rev 7: 9–17) are the martyrs and believing dead standing before God's throne in heaven.

A Multitude of Saints
before the Throne

(Rev 7:9–17 ISV)

After these things, I looked, and there was a crowd so large that no one was able to count it! They were from every nation, tribe, people, and language. They were standing in front of the throne and the lamb and were wearing white robes, with palm branches in their hands. They cried out in a loud voice, "Salvation belongs to our God, who sits on the throne, and to the lamb!" All the angels stood around the throne and around the elders and the four living creatures. They fell on their faces in front of the throne and worshipped God, saying, "Amen! Praise, glory, wisdom, thanks, honor, power, and strength be to our God forever and ever! Amen!" "Who are these people wearing white robes," one of the elders asked me, "and where did they come from?" I told him, "Sir, you know." Then he told me, "These are the people who are coming out of the terrible suffering. They have washed their robes and made them white in the blood of the lamb. That is why: "They are in front of the throne of God and worship him night and day in his Temple. The one who sits on the throne will shelter them. They will never be hungry or thirsty again. Neither the sun nor its heat will ever beat down on them, because the lamb in the center of the throne will be their shepherd. He will lead them to springs filled with the water of life, and God will wipe every tear from their eyes."

Dan 12:1b (NIV) There will be a time of distress such as has not happened from the beginning of nations until then. But at that time your people – everyone whose name is found written in the book – will be delivered.

Isa 49:10 (NIV) They will neither hunger nor thirst, nor will the desert heat or the sun beat down on them. He who has compassion on them will guide them and lead them beside springs of water.

The previous scene was on earth and relates to saints who were still alive. This scene is before God's throne and relates to saints who have died, a great multitude of people, Christians from every nation and tribe, speaking all languages and from every cultural group. They wear white robes, being clothed in the righteousness that Christ provides. They are saints who have died, and many may be tribulation martyrs. They hold palm branches in celebration of their salvation, and they sing praises to God and the Lamb who saved them.

The angel tells John that this multitude is coming out of 'the terrible suffering' or 'the great tribulation', which has not been mentioned in Revelation before and refers to the time of trouble Daniel and Jesus predicted would come at the end of the age (Dan 12:1, Matt 24:21). Jesus said that there will be *great distress unequalled from the beginning of the world until now* – and never to be equaled again. Heaven is not explicitly mentioned, but the scene is reminiscent of the heavenly throne room in chapters 4–5. Perhaps this is a vision of the resurrected saints in New Jerusalem, as there are many parallels with Revelation 21–22. The saints are before the throne of God and serve him day and night (Rev 22:3). God wipes every tear from their eyes (Rev 21:4), and he leads them to springs of living water (Rev 21:6). There is no more suffering there, the saints are protected and fully satisfied, they have entered eternal life.

The Messiah Opens the Final Seal

(Rev 8:1–6 ISV)

When the lamb opened the seventh seal, there was silence in heaven for about half an hour. Then I saw the seven angels who stand in God's presence, and seven trumpets were given to them. Another angel came with a gold censer and stood at the altar. He was given a large quantity of incense to offer on the gold altar before the throne, along with the prayers of all the saints. The smoke from the incense and the prayers of the saints went up from the angel's hand to God. The angel took the censer, filled it with fire from the altar, and threw it on the earth. Then there were peals of thunder, noises, flashes of lightning, and an earthquake. The seven angels who had the seven trumpets got ready to blow them.

When the seventh seal is opened, the contents are revealed. We have come to the climax of the world's destiny. There is silence in heaven for half an hour to mark its significance. We are not told anything yet; but the worship has ceased in anticipation of the climax, which of course, is the coming of the Messiah to establish his kingdom on earth.

Meanwhile seven angels are given trumpets to blow. Trumpets are used to make announcements. If the four horsemen represent the destructive forces of sword, famine, plague and wild beasts, the first four trumpets announce the effect they have on the world, and the latter trumpets describe the effect they have on unbelievers.

But the significance of prayer is made first. An angel with a golden censer, used for carrying hot coals, was given much incense, which he burned and offered to God with the prayers of the saints. Then, in answer to those prayers, the angel fills his censer with fiery coals and hurls them down to earth. Awe-inspiring peals of thunder, lightning, rumblings and an earthquake accompany the judgments.

Apart from God and his Messiah, the saints are the most important actors in this book. They are referred to twelve times as saints, eight times as servants of God, and nine times as people dressed in white robes, or fine, bright linen. They are the faithful in the churches from all time, of which the churches of chapters 2–3 are examples. The saints are overcomers, the ones who endured; they are the recipients of God's salvation. It is their prayers that ascend to God, and it is their shed blood that God will avenge. Many are martyrs, but they will reign with the Messiah. They come from every nation, tribe, people and language, and in their millions, they constitute the population of New Jerusalem. They are the bride of Christ, and they will reign with him for ever and ever.

Trumpets announce judgments

(Rev 8:7–13 ISV)

When the first angel blew his trumpet, hail and fire were mixed with blood and thrown on the earth. One-third of the earth was burned up, one-third of the trees was burned up, and all the green grass was burned up. When the second angel blew his trumpet, something like a huge mountain burning with fire was thrown into the sea. One-third of the sea turned into blood, one-third of the creatures that were living in the sea died, and one-third of the ships was destroyed. When the third angel blew his trumpet, a huge star blazing like a torch fell from heaven. It fell on one-third of the rivers and on the springs of water. The name of the star is Wormwood. One-third of the water turned into wormwood, and many people died from the water because it had turned bitter. When the fourth angel blew his trumpet, one-third of the sun, one-third of the moon, and one-third of the stars were struck so that one-third of them turned dark. One-third of the day was kept from having light, as was the night. Then I looked, and I heard an eagle flying overhead say in a loud voice, "How terrible, how terrible, how terrible for those living on the earth, because of the blasts of the remaining trumpets that the three angels are about to blow!"

Ezek 38:22 (NIV) I will execute judgment on him (Gog) with plague and bloodshed; I will pour down torrents of rain, hailstones and burning sulfur on him and on his troops and on the many nations with him.

You have to use your imagination with these apocalyptic visions. Picture what John saw and imagine how it might be played out in the 21st century. The hail is reminiscent of the plague inflicted on Pharaoh in Exodus 9, and the prophecy against Gog in Ezekiel 38. But here blood and fire are added, and the first four trumpets announce the effect that these plagues have on the environment; the earth, the sea, the rivers and springs, and the heavenly bodies. This is the global warming we are headed for. It is judgment carried out by God's angels.

One third of the earth and its trees are burnt, and all the grass. This isn't so much the result of violent hailstorms with lightning which starts bushfires that burn one third of the earth's surface; it is more likely the result of nuclear warfare. Then one third of the sea is affected. Something *like* a huge mountain (*not* a mountain!), all ablaze, is *thrown* into the sea. Some intercontinental ballistic missiles weigh one-hundred tons. Might this be the result of great naval battles? One third of the sea becomes blood, possibly the result of a saltwater algae called "red tide". It is on the increase with global warming, increased levels of carbon dioxide and salinity, and it kills fish, even dolphins. One third of the fish will die, and one third of ships will be destroyed.

John sees a blazing meteorite falling from the sky onto rivers and springs and people die from drinking the water. Its name is Wormwood. This could represent nuclear radiation polluting water which becomes bitter and poisonous for people to drink. The fourth trumpet is followed by a reduction of one third of the light of both day and night, as one third of the sun, moon and stars is blotted out, presumably by smoke.

An eagle flying in the sky gives a warning about three more calamities. The birds of prey are going to have a feast. These latter woes fall upon "the inhabitants of the earth", the unbelievers. The following verses only speak of two woes following the fifth and sixth trumpets. But the seventh trumpet heralds the arrival of the kingdom and the defeat of the wicked coalition. For unbelievers this will be a time of terror and judgment, the third woe.

Torturing Unbelievers
for Five Months

(Rev 9:1–6 ISV)

When the fifth angel blew his trumpet, I saw a star that had fallen to earth from the sky. The star was given the key to the shaft of the bottomless pit. It opened the shaft of the bottomless pit, and smoke came out of the shaft like the smoke from a large furnace. The sun and the air were darkened with the smoke from the shaft. Locusts came out of the smoke onto the earth, and they were given power like that of earthly scorpions. They were told not to harm the grass on the earth, any green plant, or any tree. They could harm only the people who do not have the seal of God on their foreheads. They were not allowed to kill them, but were only allowed to torture them for five months. Their torture was like the pain of a scorpion when it stings someone. In those days people will seek death, but never find it. They will long to die, but death will escape them.

Joel 1:4, 2:10–11 (NIV) What the locust swarm has left the great locusts have eaten; what the great locusts have eaten the young locusts have eaten; what the young locusts have left other locusts have eaten. … Before them the earth shakes, the heavens tremble, the sun and moon are darkened, and the stars no longer shine. The LORD thunders at the head of his army; his forces are beyond number, and mighty is the army that obeys his command. The day of the LORD is great; it is dreadful. Who can endure it?

The star which falls from heaven to earth may be Satan (Rev 12:9) or the angel of the Abyss known as Abaddon (Apollyon in Greek), which means Destroyer, or the destroying angel who is referred to several times in the Old Testament. He is given the key to the Abyss, which in ancient cosmology was the dwelling place of demons (Luke 8:31, Rev 20:1) in the depths of the sea. As the Abyss and demons are not part of the physical creation, the actions described here are symbolical rather than literal, but no less real. Smoke pours forth into the world, maybe from volcanoes or from warfare, and it darkens the sun and the sky. The world during these final years will be a frightening place to live. Compare the fifth bowl that is poured out on the throne of the Antichrist (Rev 16:10), resulting in his kingdom being plunged into darkness.

Out of the smoke appear locusts, which are a symbol of destruction. Joel 2:1–11 pictures locusts as a large and mighty army, which sound more like myriads of tanks leaping over the hills, with their firepower leaving destruction behind them. The following verses suggest that that this is the meaning here. These are not literal locusts which eat vegetation, nor are we told that they are demons. The pain they inflict is like a scorpion sting, one of the severest pains known to man. A modern non-lethal crowd-control weapon is a Pulsed Energy Projectile or PEP which produces a high level of pain. The torment is directed to the unbelievers, who don't have God's seal, for a period of five months. This means that God's servants are still there; they haven't been raptured. The unbelievers will long to die to escape the torment, but death will elude them. The sun and the sky will be darkened by smoke. Jesus said that immediately after the troubles of those days, the sun and moon will be darkened, the stars will (appear to) fall from the sky, and the powers of heaven will be shaken or disturbed (Matt 24:29).

An Army as Numerous as Locusts

(Rev 9:7–12 ISV)

The locusts looked like horses prepared for battle. On their heads were victor's crowns that looked like gold, and their faces were like human faces. They had hair like women's hair and teeth like lions' teeth. They had breastplates like iron, and the noise of their wings was like the roar of chariots with many horses rushing into battle. They had tails and stingers like scorpions, and they had the power to hurt people with their tails for five months. They had the angel of the bottomless pit ruling over them as king. In Hebrew he is called Abaddon, and in Greek he is called Apollyon. The first catastrophe is over. After these things, there are still two more catastrophes to come.

Joel 1:6 (NIV) A nation has invaded my land, a mighty army without number; it has the teeth of a lion, the fangs of a lioness.

Joel 2:2–5a (NIV) A day of darkness and gloom, a day of clouds and blackness. Like dawn spreading across the mountains a large and mighty army comes, such as never was in ancient times nor ever will be in ages to come. Before them fire devours, behind them a flame blazes. Before them the land is like the garden of Eden, behind them a desert waste – nothing escapes them. They have the appearance of horses; they gallop along like cavalry. With a noise like that of chariots they leap over the mountaintops, like a crackling fire consuming stubble, like a mighty army drawn up for battle.

Locusts don't have a king or leader; we are not talking about literal locusts, but an army of another kind. They look like horses prepared for battle. The crowns of gold mean they are out to conquer and the human faces mean they are controlled by men. They have long hair (antennae), and teeth like lions; they are cruel and inhumane (Joel 1:6). In Joel 2:4–5 their breastplates of iron and thundering noise fit a description of armored tanks. Their tails may be guns, that cause destruction and inflict pain.

The army of locusts in Joel 2 is a harbinger of the great and dreadful day of the Lord (Joel 2:31), when the Lord gathers the nations to the Valley of Jehoshaphat to enter into judgment against them (Joel 3:2).

The Antichrist is called the beast that comes up from the Abyss (Rev 11:7) and John sees the beast coming out of the sea (Rev 13:1). Some believed the Abyss or bottomless pit was to be found in the depths of the sea. It seems that this angel of the Abyss, the destroying angel, will use the armies of the Antichrist to bring about this torment on unbelievers.

The events following the fifth bowl (Rev 16:10) cover the same events that follow the fifth trumpet, but it is described in a different way. When the fifth bowl is poured out on the throne of the beast, his kingdom is plunged into darkness. Men gnaw their tongues in agony, but it is not stated what is the source of their pain. The common points are the presence of the Antichrist, the darkness, and the excruciating pain experienced by unbelievers.

An Army of Two-hundred Million Kills a Third of Humanity

(Rev 9:13–21 ISV)

> When the sixth angel blew his trumpet, I heard a voice from the four horns of the gold altar in front of God. It told the sixth angel who had the trumpet, "Release the four angels who are held at the great Euphrates River." So the four angels who were ready for that hour, day, month, and year were released to kill one-third of humanity. The number of cavalry troops was 200,000,000. I heard how many there were. This was how I saw the horses in my vision: The riders wore breastplates that had the color of fire, sapphire, and sulfur. The heads of the horses were like lions' heads, and fire, smoke, and sulfur came out of their mouths. By these three plagues—the fire, the smoke, and the sulfur that came out of their mouths—one-third of humanity was killed. For the power of these horses is in their mouths and their tails. Their tails have heads like snakes, which they use to inflict pain. The rest of the people who survived these plagues did not repent from their evil actions or stop worshiping demons and idols made of gold, silver, bronze, stone, and wood, which cannot see, hear, or walk. They did not repent from their murders, their witchcraft, their sexual immorality, or their thefts.

The release of four demons who were bound at the Euphrates River reminds us that there are demonic forces behind these events. The Euphrates River is in Iraq, and this passage should be compared with Revelation 16:12, where the sixth angel pours out his bowl on the great river Euphrates, and its water is dried up to prepare the way for the kings from the East.

Here, after the blowing of the sixth trumpet, two-hundred million troops, mounted on horses, are released at the Euphrates River. One third of mankind is killed by the fire, smoke and sulfur that come out of the mouths of their "horses".

The red, blue and yellow breastplates match the colors of fire, smoke and sulfur which comes out of the horses' mouths. John is seeing a vision of modern-day warfare; the horses and their riders may be tanks and their drivers. The lion's head symbolizes cruelty and destruction. The power in their mouths and tails are no doubt guns, fore and aft. As one third of mankind are killed, the warfare must be nuclear. The context fits that of Ezekiel 38, which is an attack on a regathered nation of Israel (Ezek 38:16) by hordes from the north, descendants of Japheth (Gen 10:2–5), and the south.

The pouring out of the sixth bowl (Rev 16:12–16) gives us more details of this battle. Demons are sent out by Satan, the Antichrist and the false prophet to gather *the kings of the whole world* for the battle on the great day of God Almighty. The place of the battle is identified as Armageddon (Rev 16:16) in Israel. Many of these leaders come from the east (Rev 16:12), and they will gather their armies under the Antichrist to make war against Jerusalem (Joel 3:2, Zech 14:2).

Dan 11:36–45 is interpreted by many to refer to the Antichrist, and if so, the southern and northern kings will come not only to attack Jerusalem, but also to fight against the Antichrist. The world's Muslims are sworn enemies of Israel with a vehement desire to destroy the State of Israel. Over one billion Muslims live east of the Euphrates river, and many of them have travelled to fight in Iraq and Syria. There are radical Islamic cells in almost every province of Indonesia.

The similarity with the Egyptian plagues during the Exodus suggests that the purpose is that people might repent of their stubbornness and idolatry, but rebellious mankind will not repent of their habitual sins summarized as idolatry (false worship), corruption, murder, and shameless immorality.

An Angel Announces
Messiah's Rule

(Rev 10:1–7 ISV)

Then I saw another powerful angel come down from heaven. He was dressed in a cloud, and there was a rainbow over his head. His face was like the sun, and his legs were like columns of fire. He held a small, opened scroll in his hand. Setting his right foot on the sea and his left foot on the land, he shouted in a loud voice as a lion roars. When he shouted, the seven thunders spoke with voices of their own. When the seven thunders spoke, I was going to write, but I heard a voice from heaven say, "Seal up what the seven thunders have said, and don't write it down." Then the angel whom I saw standing on the sea and on the land raised his right hand to heaven. He swore an oath by the one who lives forever and ever, who created heaven and everything in it, the earth and everything in it, and the sea and everything in it: "There will be no more delay. When the time approaches for the seventh angel to blow his trumpet, God's secret plan will be fulfilled, as he had announced to his servants, the prophets."

Gen 9:9–12 (NIV) I now establish my covenant with you and with your descendants after you and with every living creature that was with you – the birds, the livestock and all the wild animals, all those that came out of the ark with you – every living creature on earth. I establish my covenant with you. Never again will all life be cut off by the waters of a flood; never again will there be a flood to destroy the earth. And God said, "This is the sign of the covenant I am making between me and you and every living creature with you, a covenant for all generations to come: I have set my rainbow in the clouds, and it will be the sign of the covenant between me and the earth."

We don't know the identity of this majestic angel; only that he is a messenger from God who announces that there will be no more delay. God's redemptive purpose as announced by the Old Testament prophets is about to be fulfilled with the sounding of the seventh trumpet. When the trumpet sounds (Rev 11:15), we are told that the kingdom of the world will become the kingdom of our Lord and of his Christ, and he will reign for ever and ever. The Messiah will then reign on earth as announced by the prophets (Isa 9:6–7).

The rainbow is symbolic of God's faithfulness to his covenant with creation. He promised never again to destroy creation with a worldwide flood as he did in Noah's day (Gen 9:18). The angel's legs are like fiery pillars, which recalls the pillar of fire that guided and protected Israel during their exodus from Egypt and their desert wanderings.

The little scroll is smaller than the scroll of destiny of the world (Rev 5:1). This one contains details of the final three and a half years of that destiny. The angel roars like a lion to make his awesome, terrifying announcement. It is an act of judgment as well as an act of redemption. He stands above sea and land, emphasizing the total creation, or maybe the sea represents the nations and the land, Israel. He swears by God who lives forever and who created everything. The seven thunders sound from God's throne (Rev 4:5, 8:5, 11:19, 16:18) and express a decree of God which John was told to seal up. Daniel was also told to seal up a vision he had which concerned the Antichrist and his destruction of the holy people in the distant future (Dan 8:26). Thunder expresses a warning that God's anger is about to burst forth in judgment. The majestic angel is announcing the end of the world as we know it. There will be fearful destruction and at least a third of mankind will die, but the world and God's people will survive.

Glorification will Follow Suffering

(Rev 10:8–11 ISV)

Then the voice that I had heard from heaven spoke to me again, saying, "Go and take the opened scroll from the hand of the angel who is standing on the sea and on the land." So I went to the angel and asked him to give me the small scroll. "Take it and eat it," he told me. "It will turn bitter in your stomach, but it will be as sweet as honey in your mouth." So I took the small scroll from the angel's hand and ate it. It was as sweet as honey in my mouth, but when I had eaten it, it turned bitter in my stomach. Then the seven thunders told me, "You must prophesy again about many peoples, nations, languages, and kings."

Ps 119:103 (NIV) How sweet are your words to my taste, sweeter than honey to my mouth!

Ezek 2:8 – 3:3 (NIV) But you, son of man, listen to what I say to you. Do not rebel like that rebellious people; open your mouth and eat what I give you. Then I looked, and I saw a hand stretched out to me. In it was a scroll, which he unrolled before me. On both sides of it were written words of lament and mourning and woe. And he said to me, "Son of man, eat what is before you, eat this scroll; then go and speak to the people of Israel." So I opened my mouth, and he gave me the scroll to eat. Then he said to me, "Son of man, eat this scroll I am giving you and fill your stomach with it. So I ate it, and it tasted as sweet as honey in my mouth."

At the beginning of his ministry, the prophet Ezekiel was offered a scroll to eat and it wasn't a sweet coffee scroll! It contained words of lament and mourning and woe, but it tasted sweet to him because it was the word of God. John, on the other hand, ate a smaller scroll which tasted sweet to him, perhaps for the same reason, but afterwards he had a stomach ache. The sweetness was also because of the glorious outcome, the coming of the Messiah and the establishing of his kingdom upon the earth. But it resulted in a stomach ache when he realized all the suffering God's people would have to go through before that glorious day. You can read through the book of Revelation and rejoice that Jesus is coming back and that he will have total victory over evil. But when you get into it more deeply, you will notice that the saints are handed over to the Antichrist for three and a half years. They are not taken out of the world before the trouble begins, and it is clear that there will be many Christian martyrs. That is why John got his stomach ache.

When Ezekiel ate his scroll, he was told to go to the house of Israel and speak God's word to them. He was also told to enact a siege of Jerusalem, as a warning to Israel. That event will be repeated during the Great Tribulation, so John's visions (Rev 11–12) seem to relate especially to Israel and the people of Jerusalem.

John is told he must prophesy again about many peoples, nations, languages and kings. This relates to the rest of the book of Revelation. Chapters 19–22 would have been very sweet to him, but chapters 11–18 describe the persecution that the saints will undergo under the Antichrist and the destruction and suffering the world will suffer as God pours out his wrath. Christians who understand the book of Revelation are the only people who know how this age is going to come to an end. We have an obligation therefore to study this book carefully and be witnesses to its teaching. People will increasingly want to know the answers as the time draws near.

John Measures the Temple

(Rev 11:1–2 ISV)

Then I was given a stick like a measuring rod. I was told, "Stand up and measure the Temple of God and the altar, and count those who worship there. But don't measure the courtyard outside the Temple. Leave that out, because it is given to the nations, and they will trample the Holy City for 42 months.

Dan 7:25 (NIV) He [the Antichrist] will speak against the Most High and oppress his saints and try to change the set times and the laws. The saints will be handed over to him for a time, times and half a time.

Dan 9:27 (NIV) He will confirm a covenant with many for one "seven" In the middle of the "seven" he will put an end to sacrifice and offering. And at the temple he will set up an abomination that causes desolation, until the end that is decreed is poured out on him.

Dan 12:11 (NIV) From the time that the daily sacrifice is abolished and the abominations that causes desolation is set up, there will be 1290 days.

Luke 21:24 (NIV) Jerusalem will be trampled on by the Gentiles until the times of the Gentiles are fulfilled.

This vision continues from chapter 10 and is about the nation of Israel, which became a nation on May 14th 1948, Jerusalem, which Israel declared to be its official capital in 1980, and the temple which will be rebuilt in the holy city during the first half of the tribulation after the

Antichrist has made a peace deal with Israel. Measuring the temple is a symbolic act, not to determine its dimensions, but to prophesy divine preservation of the Jewish race.

Paul prophesied that the Antichrist would set himself up in the temple, proclaiming himself to be God (2 Thess 2:4). Jesus also spoke about the time when people would see standing in the temple, the abomination that causes desolation, spoken of by the prophet Daniel (Matt 24:15). Daniel said this would happen in the middle of the tribulation period (Dan 9:27, 12:11). The Antichrist will make a covenant with "many" for seven years, and then break it half way through. He will invade it, put an end to sacrifice and offerings, and set up an image of himself in God's temple proclaiming himself to be God.

Ezekiel saw a vision of a new temple for restored Israel and a man measuring it with a rod (Ezek 40–48). Now John sees a vision of a temple and is told to go and measure it and the Jewish worshipers who were there. He is told to exclude the outer court, because it will be given over to the Gentiles, who under the Antichrist will trample the holy city for forty-two months, the second half of the tribulation (Rev 13:5). Half the city would go into exile (Zech 14:2) and God would look after them in the desert (Rev 12:6, 13–14).

The forty-two months alludes to Daniel 7:25 where it is expressed as "a time, times and half a time". During this period of three and a half years, or 1260 days, the Antichrist will slander God, his dwelling place and the inhabitants of heaven and severely persecute the saints and conquer them (Rev 13:6–7).

Satan is ejected from heaven at this time and he immediately seeks to exterminate Israel (Rev 12:13). The Antichrist will take his seat in the temple as God and demand universal worship. The false prophet will set up an image in honor of the beast in the temple and order the execution of those who don't worship him (Rev 13:14–16).

Two Christians Preach
in Jerusalem

(Rev 11:3–7 ISV)

> I will give my two witnesses who wear sackcloth the authority to prophesy for 1,260 days." These witnesses are the two olive trees and the two lamp stands standing in the presence of the Lord of the earth. And if anyone should want to hurt them, fire comes out of their mouths and burns up their enemies. If anyone wants to hurt them, he must be killed in this manner. These witnesses have authority to close the heavens in order to keep rain from falling while they are prophesying. They also have authority to turn bodies of water into blood and to strike the earth with any plague, as often as they desire. When they have finished their testimony, the beast that comes up from the bottomless pit will wage war against them, conquer them, and kill them.
>
> **Exod 7:17b** (NIV) With the staff that is in my [Moses] hand I will strike the water of the Nile, and it will be changed into blood.
>
> **1 Kings 17:1b** (NIV) As the Lord, the God of Israel, lives, whom I serve, there will be neither dew nor rain in the next few years except at my word [spoken by Elijah].
>
> **Jer 5:14** (NIV) Because the people have spoken these words, I will make my words in your mouth a fire and these people the wood it consumes.
>
> **Zech 4:3, 13** (NIV) Also there are two *olive trees* by it, one on the right of the bowl and the other on its left. ... These are the two who are anointed to serve the Lord of all the earth.
>
> **Mal 4:5** (NIV) "See, I will send the prophet Elijah to you before that great and dreadful day of the Lord comes."

The two witnesses are Christians who will proclaim God's word to Israel and the Jews in Jerusalem, where their Lord was crucified. They are metaphorically referred to as two olive trees and two lampstands. The olive oil used for anointing is symbolic of the Holy Spirit. The lampstands support lamps which burn the oil, and here symbolize two men who are empowered by God's Spirit. In Zechariah 3–4 the lampstands referred to the civil and religious leaders; the governor Zerubbabel, and the high priest Joshua, *whose job it was to complete the building of the second temple* in Jerusalem around 520 BC, and who were empowered by the Holy Spirit to do so (Zech 4:6). The two witnesses may be responsible for the rebuilding of the temple during the first half of the tribulation, but their witness is during the second half. They will be miraculously protected from harm until their ministry is finished. They will fulfil the final prophecy of the Old Testament (cf. Mal 4:5–6, Matt 17:11).

The witnesses are modelled after Moses (Exod 7:17) and Elijah (1 Kings 17:1). They will be empowered to do miracles throughout the time of their ministry, similar to the way Moses and Elijah ministered. They will dress in sackcloth to symbolize their message of repentance. Fire will come from their mouths and kill their enemies. In Elijah's case, he called down fire from heaven (2 Kings 1:9–12). They will prevent rain from falling during their ministry as Elijah did for three and a half years (James 5:17). They will turn water into blood, as Moses did, and the effect of their ministry will be felt worldwide as they have power to strike the earth with every kind of calamity at will. There will be tension between these powerful, godly preachers and the powerful, godless the Antichrist, who will overrun Jerusalem for the final three and a half years of the tribulation period. When they finish their work, the Antichrist is permitted to kill them.

The Two Witnesses Are Brought Back to Life

(Rev 11:8–14 ISV)

> Their dead bodies will lie in the street of the great city that is spiritually called Sodom and Egypt, where their Lord was crucified. For three and a half days some members of the peoples, tribes, languages, and nations will look at their dead bodies and will not allow them to be placed in a tomb. Those living on earth will gloat over them, celebrate, and send gifts to each other, because these two prophets had tormented those living on earth. But after the three and a half days, the breath of life from God entered them, and they stood on their feet. Those who watched them were terrified. Then the witnesses heard a loud voice from heaven calling to them, "Come up here!" So they went up to heaven in a cloud, and their enemies watched them. At that moment a powerful earthquake struck. One-tenth of the city collapsed, 7,000 people were killed by the earthquake, and the rest were terrified and gave glory to the God of heaven. The second catastrophe is over. The third catastrophe is coming very soon.
>
> **Isa 1:10a** (NIV) Hear the word of the LORD, you rulers of Sodom.

The setting of Revelation 11 is Jerusalem, where their Lord was crucified, figuratively called Sodom (immoral), and Egypt (oppressive). The witnesses are finally killed by the Antichrist, but after three and a half days they come back to life, stand up, and ascend to heaven. Unbelievers from every tribe and language will gaze on them (maybe on their mobile phones and televisions) and gloat over their downfall. But then there is a severe earthquake. A tenth of Jerusalem collapses and seven thousand people are killed. This would seem to be the same "severe earthquake" mentioned in Revelation 6:12 and 16:18.

The survivors of the inhabitants of Jerusalem glorify God. Giving glory to God is indicative of fearing and worshiping him (Rev 14:7), and is also bracketed with repentance (Rev 16:9). Here it prepares the way for Israel's conversion at the Messiah's return as predicted by Zechariah. The Lord will pour out on the house of David and *the inhabitants of Jerusalem* a spirit of grace and supplication. They will look on him whom they pierced (crucified), and they will mourn for him. On that day a fountain will be opened to the house of David and *the inhabitants of Jerusalem*, to cleanse then from sin and impurity (Zech 12:10, 13:1). See also Isaiah 59:20 where the Redeemer comes to Zion, to those in Jacob who repent of their sins, and Romans 11:26 where all Israel is saved, as the deliverer comes from Zion and banishes ungodliness from Jacob.

The second woe has passed; the third woe is imminent. It is probably to be identified with the events following the blowing of the seventh trumpet, the arrival of the Messiah and his total victory over the armies that have surrounded Jerusalem.

The Arrival of the Messianic Kingdom

(Rev 11:15–19 ISV)

When the seventh angel blew his trumpet, there were loud voices in heaven, saying, "The world's kingdom has become the kingdom of our Lord and of his Messiah, and he will rule forever and ever." Then the twenty-four elders who were sitting on their thrones in God's presence fell on their faces and worshipped God. They said, "We give thanks to you, Lord God Almighty, who is and who was, because you have taken your great power and have begun to rule. The nations were angry, but the time for your wrath has come. It is time for the dead to be judged— to reward your servants, the prophets, the saints, and all who fear your name, both unimportant and important, and to destroy those who destroy the earth." Then the Temple of God in heaven was opened, and the ark of his covenant was seen inside his Temple. There were flashes of lightning, noises, peals of thunder, an earthquake, and heavy hail.

Ps 2:1–2 (NIV) Why do the nations conspire, and the peoples plot in vain? The kings of the earth take their stand and the rulers gather together against the Lord and against his Anointed One.

Dan 2:44 (NIV) In the time of those kings, the God of heaven will set up a kingdom that will never be destroyed, nor will it be left to another people. It will crush all those kingdoms and bring them to an end, but it will itself endure forever.

Zech 14:9 (NIV) The Lord will be king over all the earth. On that day there will be one Lord, and his name the only name.

After the seventh trumpet is blown, a prophetic announcement is made that the kingdom of the world has become the kingdom of the Messiah. The kingdoms of the world will be destroyed together with their armies and Messiah's sovereignty will be established. The details of the destruction are given in chapter 18, where Babylon and all the cities associated with it are destroyed along with those who destroy the earth; the armies who have gathered at Armageddon.

The twenty-four elders worship the Lord in anticipation; the Messiah is about to show his great power and *begin his reign* on earth. His great power will be displayed in the final conflict against the forces of evil on the Day of the Lord. The Lord God Almighty often refers to God, but here it is the Son of Man, the Messiah, who will be king. The messianic reign begins. God always reigns on his heavenly throne. He was described before as him who is, and who was, and who is to come (Rev 1:4), but here he is simply him who is and who was, because he has come at last.

Psalm 2 is messianic and is frequently quoted in the New Testament. The Lord said he will install his king, the Messiah (Jesus), on Zion his holy hill. The nations will be his inheritance, the ends of the earth his possession. Three things are mentioned that the Messiah will do: He will judge the dead, reward the saints, and destroy the destroyers of the earth. The resurrection of the righteous effectively judges the dead; some are taken, the others are left.

God lives in a different realm to us; so references to his temple and the ark of the covenant are symbolic, not literal. They are what John saw in his vision. They symbolize the fellowship God has with his people and his faithfulness to fulfil his promises. The thunder, lighting, earthquake and hailstorm are on earth, as described in Revelation 16:17–21 when the seventh bowl is poured out.

The Birth and Ascension of the Messiah

(Rev 12:1–6 ISV)

A spectacular sign appeared in the sky: a woman dressed with the sun, who had the moon under her feet and a victor's crown of twelve stars on her head. She was pregnant and was crying out from her labor pains, the agony of giving birth. Then another sign appeared in the sky: a huge red dragon with seven heads, ten horns, and seven royal crowns on its heads. Its tail swept away one-third of the stars in the sky and knocked them down to the earth. Then the dragon stood in front of the woman who was about to give birth so that it could devour her child when it was born. She gave birth to a son, a boy, who is to rule all the nations with an iron scepter. But her child was snatched away and taken to God and to his throne. Then the woman fled into the wilderness, where a place had been prepared for her by God so that she might be taken care of for 1,260 days.

Gen 37:9 (NIV) Then he had another dream, and he told it to his brothers. "Listen," he said, "I had another dream, and this time the sun and moon and eleven stars were bowing down to me."

Ps 2:9 (NIV) You will break them with a rod of iron; you will dash them to pieces like pottery.

The cosmic drama which involves God's plan for the world is a spiritual battle in the heavenly realm between God and Satan. Satan gained power over humanity through the sin of Adam and Eve. Understanding this drama helps us understand the spiritual significance of persecution.

In the past, Satan set out to destroy the baby Messiah; in the future he will seek to abort Messiah's reign on earth by destroying God's people, both Christians and Israel. There will be many martyrs, but not a hair of their heads will perish.

In this vision, John sees a woman who gives birth to a child who will rule the nations with an iron scepter. An enormous red dragon plans to devour the child, but he fails. The ten horns and seven crowns symbolize his power and authority. The woman flees to the desert to be protected by God for 1,260 days. The child is Jesus, the Messiah. It is he who will rule the nations rigorously with an iron scepter (Ps 2:9, Rev 19:15). The mother is not Mary, but Israel, depicted symbolically, as in Joseph's dream (Gen 37:9–11). The red dragon is Satan (verse 9), who through the edict of Herod, tried to kill the baby Jesus. Jesus was taken up to God at the ascension. The 1,260 days relate to the last three and a half years of this age, when Israel will be oppressed by the Antichrist and his worldwide empire.

Verse 4 speaks of the devil sweeping one third of the stars from heaven to earth. Obviously, they are not literal stars, and most commentators believe they are the fallen angels. Jesus said that an eternal fire had been prepared for the devil and his angels (Matt 25:41). These "angels" are what we would call evil spirits or demons. Jude 6 speaks of them as angels who didn't keep their own position but abandoned their assigned place. Cf. Isa 14:12–14, Luke 10:18.

God will protect Israel in an uninhabited place for 1260 days after Satan is thrown down to earth. This is described in the following section. It is the same forty-two-month period during which the Gentiles trample on the holy city and the time when the Antichrist oppresses God's people (Rev 13:5).

SATAN AND HIS DEMONS DRIVEN OUT OF HEAVEN

(REV 12:7–12 ISV)

Then a war broke out in heaven. Michael and his angels fought with the dragon, and the dragon and its angels fought back. But it was not strong enough, and there was no longer any place for them in heaven. The huge dragon was hurled down. That ancient serpent, called the Devil and Satan, the deceiver of the whole world, was hurled down to the earth, along with its angels. Then I heard a loud voice in heaven say, "Now the salvation, the power, the kingdom of our God, and the authority of his Messiah have come. For the one who accuses our brothers, who accuses them day and night in the presence of our God, has been thrown out. Our brothers conquered him by the blood of the lamb and by the word of their testimony, for they did not cling to their lives even in the face of death. So be glad, heavens, and those who live in them! How terrible it is for the earth and the sea, because the Devil has come down to you, filled with rage, knowing that his time is short!"

Dan 12:1 (NIV) At that time Michael, the great prince who protects your people, will arise. There will be a time of distress such as has not happened from the beginning of nations until then. But at that time your people – everyone whose name is found written in the book – will be delivered.

There is war in heaven! Victory over Satan in the heavenly realm will precede the victory of Israel over her enemies on earth. The archangel Michael, who is the protector of Israel (Dan 12:1), is at war against Satan, who is out to destroy Israel. The nation of Israel is loved by God because of the patriarchs, for God's gifts and his call are irrevocable (Rom 11:28–29). Satan is defeated and loses his place in heaven. This evil angel, who leads the whole world astray, is hurled down to earth together with his demons. This expulsion of Satan from heaven happens three and a half years before the end of the age. His time on earth is short, and it will result in the final deliverance of God's people, in a great manifestation of God's power, and in the establishment of his kingdom on earth, under the authority of the Messiah.

Two thirds of Jews will lose their lives (Zech 13:8–9) and an unknown number of Christians, but in those final days, faith will be more important than life. Victory over Satan will be accomplished primarily because of the cross and the blood that Christ shed on their behalf, but also because of the faithful testimony that Christians will bear in the face of persecution and martyrdom.

Jesus said that there will be great distress, unequaled from the beginning of the world and never to be equaled again. He said if those days hadn't been reduced, *no one would survive*, but for the sake of the elect those days will be reduced (Matt 24:21–22). Knowing he only has a short time, Satan, in his fury, will bring much destruction to the earth and the sea, as a result of warfare that he instigates (Rev 16:13–14).

Satan Persecutes Israel and the Church

(Rev 12:13-17 ISV)

When the dragon saw that it had been thrown down to the earth, it pursued the woman who had given birth to the boy. However, the woman was given the two wings of a large eagle so that she could fly away from the serpent to her place in the wilderness, where she could be taken care of for a time, times, and half a time. From its mouth the serpent spewed water like a river behind the woman in order to sweep her away with the flood. But the earth helped the woman by opening its mouth and swallowing the river that the dragon had spewed from its mouth. The dragon became angry with the woman and went away to do battle against the rest of her children, the ones who keep God's commandments and hold on to the testimony about Jesus. Then the dragon stood on the sand of the seashore.

Exod 19:4 (NIV) You yourselves have seen what I did to Egypt, and how I carried you on eagles' wings and brought you to myself.

When Satan is banished to the earth, his first inclination is to destroy Israel. The river of water that he spews in their direction is a wave of persecution, comparable to that of the Nazis. Some people interpret the woman as being the church, but it wasn't the church who gave birth to Jesus. The eagles' wings give us a clue that she is Israel (Exod 19:4). The Lord brought Israel from Egypt into the Sinai desert "on eagles' wings", and at the end he is going to look after them again, during those 1260 days of tribulation, the time of Jacob's trouble. It will be an awful time, especially for Israel, but Israel will be saved out of it (Jer 30:7). There is a place in the wilderness that God has prepared for Israel during the three and a half years of Satan's rage and the Antichrist's oppression. Just where that might be, nobody knows.

The *earth* that will help the woman may refer to the inhabitants of the world. It could mean something like the United Nations deciding in favor of Israel, as they did on May 14th, 1948, when Israel became a modern nation (Isa 66:7–8). Or the United States may come to the rescue, or neighboring Jordan.

When Satan fails in his effort to exterminate Israel, he turns on the other offspring of Judaism, the church, those who obey God's commandments and hold to the testimony that Jesus bore. In other words, Bible believing Christians who are committed to Jesus. We read about how he makes war on the saints in chapter 13.

The dragon, Satan, is seen standing by the sea, because he is about to empower an international world government that will include all coastlands and islands of the sea.

The Rise of the Final World Empire

(Rev 13:1–4 ISV)

> I saw a beast coming out of the sea. It had ten horns, seven heads, and ten royal crowns on its horns. On its heads were blasphemous names. The beast that I saw was like a leopard. Its feet were like bear's feet, and its mouth was like a lion's mouth. The dragon gave it his power, his throne, and complete authority. One of the beast's heads looked like it had sustained a mortal wound, but its fatal wound was healed. Rapt with amazement, the whole world followed the beast. They worshipped the dragon because it had given authority to the beast. They also worshipped the beast, saying, "Who is like the beast, and who can fight a war with it?"
>
> **Dan 7:7** (NIV) After that, in my vision at night I looked, and there before me was a fourth beast – terrifying and frightening and very powerful. It had large iron teeth; it crushed and devoured its victims and trampled underfoot whatever was left. It was different from all the former beasts and it had ten horns.
>
> **Dan 7:23–24a** (NIV) He gave me this explanation: "The fourth beast is a fourth kingdom that will appear on earth. It will be different from all the other kingdoms and will devour the *whole earth*, trampling it down and crushing it. The ten horns are ten kings who will come from this kingdom."

The beast comes out of the Abyss (11:7, 17:8), which was believed to be located in the deepest sea. The beast mentioned in verses 1–4 is not a man; it is a worldwide empire as described in Daniel 7. This beast from the sea is an international coalition of countries; political globalization. Satanically empowered, it will be overtly anti-Christian and anti-Jewish. It has seven heads and ten horns just like the dragon who empowers it. The whole world will be deceived by its ideology. This empire will be oppressive, violent, blasphemous and dictatorial. The crowns are on the horns rather than the heads, they are symbolic of power. The crowned horns are leaders. "Ten" may simply express the comprehensiveness of this global coalition. The seven heads are interpreted as seven hills (Rev 17:9–10), but they are also seven kings. The Roman empire existed for over one thousand years and included parts of north Africa and the Middle east. Rome itself was built on seven hills, suggesting that the final world empire is a revived Roman empire.

One of the heads of the beast had a fatal wound which was healed, a way of saying that the empire ceased to exist for some time and then was resurrected (Rev 17:8). The statue that Daniel saw in chapter 2 had legs of iron (Rome, being the fourth empire, stretched from Britain to Iraq), and ten toes that were part iron and part clay. The legs and toes all represent the same world empire, the toes symbolizing the unstable confederation of nations in the end times.

The final world empire will involve political, economic and cultural globalization of which the UN will surely have a key role. The whole world will be full of wonder which becomes worship. They will embrace it, submit to its laws, and will worship Satan, the power behind it. Just as the Father gave Jesus authority over the whole world, so Satan will give his power, throne and authority to the leader of this final empire. According to Daniel, this world government will be very frightening; powerful, violent, destructive and despotic, even before the rise of the Antichrist (Dan 7:8, Rev 13:5).

The Antichrist Opposes
God and the Saints

(Rev 13:5–8 ISV)

The beast was allowed to speak arrogant and blasphemous things, and it was given authority for 42 months. It uttered blasphemies against God, against his name, and against his residence, that is, against those who are living in heaven. It was allowed to wage war against the saints and to conquer them. It was also given authority over every tribe, people, language, and nation. All those who had become settled down and at home, living on the earth, will worship it, everyone whose name had not been written in the Book of Life belonging to the lamb that had been slaughtered since the foundation of the world.

Dan 7:8 (NIV) While I was thinking about the horns, there before me was another horn, a little one, which came up among them; and three of the first horns were uprooted before it. This horn had eyes like the eyes of aa human being and a mouth that spoke boastfully.

Dan 7:21 (NIV) As I watched, this horn was waging war against the holy people and defeating them.

Dan 7:24b–25 (NIV) After them another king will arise, different from the earlier ones; he will subdue three kings. He will speak against the Most High and oppress his holy people and try to change the set times and the laws. The holy people will be delivered into his hands for a time, times and half time.

Dan 11:36 (NIV) The king will do as he pleases. He will exalt and magnify himself above every god and will say unheard of things against the God of gods. He will be successful until the time of wrath is completed, for what has been determined must take place.

The beast in these verses no longer refers to the empire, but to its infamous leader, the Antichrist. He is regularly called the beast in Revelation but is commonly known as the Antichrist. He is the "mouth" given to the beast, to utter proud words and blasphemies and to exercise his authority for forty-two months. He is described as a man of lawlessness who opposes and exalts himself over everything that is called God or is worshiped (2 Thess 2:4). He even sets himself up in God's temple, proclaiming himself to be God. In Daniel 7:8 he is described as a little horn (an insignificant leader) who rises to power by defeating three other leaders. He will lead this empire that will rule the world during the final years before the Messiah's return. He will vehemently oppose all worship – except for himself. He has eyes (intelligence) and a mouth (arrogance). He will embody satanic evil and have great military and political power.

The Antichrist will wage war against the saints and defeat them (Dan 7:21, Rev 13:7). This will be the most intense and extensive persecution that the church has ever undergone. If God had not informed us about what is to come, it would have been a very confusing time for Christians. But God has warned us, and told us to be patient and faithful, even unto death. The Antichrist will be a world dictator, more powerful than Hitler. He will have authority over every tribe, people, language and nation. Everyone will be forced to worship him, and to submit to his satanically inspired authority. Only those whose names are written in the Lamb's book of life will have the courage to disobey him, at the cost of their lives.

The phrase "from the creation of the world" relates to the book of life, as it does in Revelation 17:8, rather the Lamb that was slain. Jesus' death was decreed by God from eternity, but it happened in time, when Jesus was crucified.

The Saints will Require Endurance

(Rev 13:9–10 ISV)

Let everyone listen: If anyone is to be taken captive, into captivity he will go. If anyone is to be killed with a sword, with a sword he will be killed. Here is a call for endurance and faith of the saints:

Jer 15:2 (NIV) And if they ask you, "Where shall we go?" tell them, this is what the LORD says: "Those destined for death, to death; those for the sword, to the sword; those for starvation, to starvation; those for captivity, to captivity."

This call for patience and endurance and faithfulness on the part of the saints is repeated in Revelation 14:12–13. It is one of the most important themes in the book. The elect are those who obey God. They are not ignorant of his eternal plan to save believers through their faith in Christ. When facing imprisonment or martyrdom in the final days, they will find courage and strength to be loyal to their Lord. After all, to turn from the Lord and submit to the Antichrist would in reality be to worship Satan.

If we are there, the Lord will expect us to be faithful and brave. That time will be extremely difficult, a real test of faith, and only the elect will have the courage to disobey the Antichrist and be victorious. On that day our faith will enable us to overcome. How could we submit to the instructions of the Antichrist or the false prophet, who are both inspired by Satan? How could we bow down and worship him, or allow the number of his name to be stamped on our bodies? On dying, our spirits will go to be with the Lord (2 Cor 5:8), and a short time later our bodies will be resurrected, and we will rule the world with the Messiah. In the last years of the Great Tribulation, there will be no reason for Christians to remain in the condemned world; death will be preferable.

Suffering for Christ's sake and believing in him are both gifts or privileges that God has given us (Phil 1:29). As Christians, we can expect both an abundance of suffering for his sake and also an abundance of comfort (2 Cor 1:5). We share in his sufferings so that we can share in his glory (Rom 8:17). Paul said he wanted to know Christ and his resurrection power better, by sharing in his sufferings even to the point of death (Phil 3:10). We must go through many hardships to enter the kingdom of God (Acts 14:22).

The False Prophet

(Rev 13:11–18 ISV)

I saw another beast coming up out of the earth. It had two horns like a lamb and it talked like a dragon. It uses all the authority of the first beast on its behalf, and it makes the earth and those living on it worship the first beast, whose mortal wound was healed. It performs spectacular signs, even making fire come down from heaven to earth in front of people. It deceives those living on earth with the signs that it is allowed to do on behalf of the first beast, telling them to make an image for the beast who was wounded by a sword and yet lived. The second beast was allowed to impart life to the image of the first beast so that the image of the beast could talk and order the execution of those who would not worship the image of the beast. The second beast forces all people—important and unimportant, rich and poor, free and slaves—to be marked on their right hands or on their foreheads, so that no one may buy or sell unless he has the mark, which is the beast's name or the number of its name. In this case wisdom is needed: Let the person who has understanding calculate the total number of the beast, because it is a human total number, and the sum of the number is 666.

Matt 24:24 (NIV) For false messiahs and false prophets will appear and perform great signs and wonders to deceive, if possible, even the elect.

2 Thess 2:9, 10a (NIV) The coming of the lawless one will be in accordance with how Satan works. He will use all sorts of displays of power through signs and wonders that serve the lie, and all the ways that wickedness deceives those who are perishing.

John sees another beast coming out of the earth. Empires rise from the sea, but men rise from the earth. This beast is not an empire, but a man, a bestial man. He will appear gentle like a lamb, but he will speak like a dragon. He is a deceiver who will perform miracles with satanic power. He is closely associated with the Antichrist, who is also called the beast (Rev 13:14), and he will instruct everyone to worship him and be branded with his mark, a sign of allegiance. He will order people to set up an image of the Antichrist which he will animate, so that it can speak. This is the abomination that causes desolation standing in the holy place (Matt 24:15). Paul said the lawless one will set himself up in God's temple and proclaim himself to be God (2 Thess 2:4). Anyone who refuses to worship the image will be executed. Everyone, whether rich or poor, will be forced to receive a mark on the right hand or forehead. Without the mark, nobody will be able to buy or sell anything.

The mark is 666. Nobody can identify the name it represents yet. It is the name of the beast, that is, the Antichrist's name. 666 is the sum of his name. Deriving numbers from names is a practice called gematria. As Revelation is written in Greek, we need to think in terms of Greek spelling. For example, Jesus in Greek is Ιησούς. Ι = 10, η = 8, σ = 200, ο = 70, ύ = 400, ς = 200. The number of Jesus' name is 888.

This second beast is otherwise called the false prophet (Rev 16:13, 19:20, 20:10), because he is a religious figure. He will perform miracles and oppose all religion except his own. He will exalt the Antichrist over everything that is called God or is worshiped, and he will execute those who disobey his orders.

The word "antichrist" does not occur in the book of Revelation. He is mentioned in John's letters (1 John 2:18, 22, 4:3, 2 John 7), where he is depicted as a religious deceiver or an adversary of the Messiah. Paul calls him the lawless one. In Revelation he is referred to as the beast over thirty times. Satan, the Antichrist, and the false prophet are a triumvirate, the evil equivalent of the Holy Trinity.

The Messiah and the Saints Standing on Mount Zion

(Rev 14:1–5 ISV)

Then I looked, and there was the lamb, standing on Mount Zion! With him were 144,000 people who had his name and his Father's name written on their foreheads. Then I heard a sound from heaven like that of many waters and like the sound of loud thunder. The sound I heard was like harpists playing on their harps. They were singing a new song in front of the throne, the four living creatures, and the elders. No one could learn the song except the 144,000 who had been redeemed from the earth. They have not defiled themselves with women, for they are virgins, and they follow the lamb wherever he goes. They have been redeemed from among humanity as the first fruits for God and the lamb. In their mouth no lie was found. They are blameless.

Ps 2:6 (NIV) I have installed my King on Zion, my holy mountain.

Joel 2:32 (NIV) And everyone who calls on the name of the Lord will be saved; for on Mount Zion and in Jerusalem there will be deliverance, as the Lord has said, even among the survivors whom the Lord calls.

Jer 2:3 (NIV) Israel was holy to the Lord, the first fruits of his harvest.

Zeph 3:13 (NIV) The remnant of Israel will do no wrong; they will speak no lies, nor will deceit be found in their mouths.

Mount Zion was also called the City of David, and it became synonymous with Jerusalem. Here we have the victorious Messiah standing with the saints, those who had been sealed with the seal of the living God (Rev 7:2). This scene contrasts the state of the saints with the unbelievers in chapter 13 who received the mark of the beast. The Messiah has not arrived on earth yet; this vision takes place in the throne room of heaven with the living creatures and the elders. The Mount Zion John sees is the heavenly Jerusalem (Heb 12:22), the holy city which will come down out of heaven, so that the Lamb might rule over the world together with the victorious church. There is loud joyful music playing as the saints sing a new song. These are the overcomers who have successfully passed through the Great Tribulation. The words of the new song they sing may be the same as those sung by the living creatures and the elders in Revelation 5:9–10 or 15:3–4.

The saints are described as virgins. This word picture distinguishes them as being morally pure and faithful. They didn't worship the Antichrist or receive his mark on their bodies. They follow Jesus, the great Shepherd of the sheep, wherever he goes. They are honest and blameless. They are now perfected, and their sins are forgiven. Their way of life is in marked contrast to that of the evildoers (Rev 22:15).

They have been redeemed and they are offered to God and Jesus as a choice offering. Both the harvest of the righteous (the first fruits – Rev 14:14–16) and the harvest of the wicked (Rev 14:17–20) are described in symbolic language. The righteous are an acceptable offering, redeemed from the inhabitants of the earth, and purchased from among all mankind with the blood of Christ (1 Pet 1:18–19).

The Gospel Preached
to All Nations

(Rev 14:6–8 ISV)

> Then I saw another angel flying overhead with the eternal gospel to proclaim to those who live on earth—to every nation, tribe, language, and people. He said in a loud voice, "Fear God and give him glory, because the time for him to judge has arrived. Worship the one who made heaven and earth, the sea and springs of water." Then another angel, a second one, followed him, saying, "Fallen! Babylon the Great has fallen! She has made all nations drink the wine, the wrath earned for her sexual sins."
>
> **Isa 21:9** (NIV) Babylon has fallen, has fallen! All the images of its gods lie shattered on the ground.

Chapter 13 informed us about the satanically inspired final world empire, and the false prophet who will enforce his message on everyone: to worship the Antichrist and submit to his government.

Chapter 14 started with an interlude about the Messiah and the saints, who didn't defile themselves with the pagan world system, and who are now in heaven.

This is now followed by three angels who warn about impending judgment, before a symbolic description of the harvest of the earth, of both the righteous and then the wicked. It is difficult to envisage three angels preaching the gospel in mid-air to unbelievers on earth, so we need to interpret these angels as messengers who symbolize the church with her message of eternal salvation through faith in Christ, acceptance of which is the only way to escape the impending judgment of the world. John saw the angels flying in mid-air, for all to see, proclaiming the gospel to every nation, tribe, language and people. This is in fulfilment of the Lord's promise (Matt 24:14) that the gospel would be preached in the whole world, by the church, as a witness to all nations, and then the end would come.

The only way of escape is to fear God and give him glory, to recognize that he is the Creator of all things, and that one day he will judge everyone according to what they have done. Belief in the good news about Jesus Christ is not explicitly mentioned, but it is implicit in the word "gospel" which means "good news".

The messages of the three "messengers" are related. The first gives the invitation to all to believe in the gospel, the second announces the fall of the rebellious world system with its luxuries and moral decadence, while the third warns that everyone who worships the Antichrist will share in his judgment and suffer eternal punishment in hell. As many Christians are martyred, the whole world will look on, and the church will preach its message.

The second angel announces the fall of Babylon. Historically Babylon was the arch-enemy of Israel, the powerful empire that conquered Jerusalem in 587 BC, destroyed Solomon's temple, and took the Jewish people and their king into exile. The name is used here symbolically of the last world empire associated with the Antichrist. The angel, by quoting Isaiah's prophecy that Babylon has fallen, is announcing that God is about to overthrow the rebellious civilization that has been a willing accomplice with the Antichrist and the false prophet, who have intoxicated the world with their corruption and idolatry.

Beware of Worshiping the Antichrist

(Rev 14:9–13 ISV)

Then another angel, a third one, followed them, saying in a loud voice, "Whoever worships the beast and its image and receives a mark on his forehead or his hand will drink the wine of God's wrath, which has been poured undiluted into the cup of his anger. He will be tortured with fire and sulfur in the presence of the holy angels and the lamb. The smoke from their torture goes up forever and ever. There is no rest day or night for those who worship the beast and its image or for anyone who receives the mark of its name." Here is a call for the endurance of the saints, who keep the commandments of God and hold fast to their faithfulness in Jesus: I heard a voice from heaven say, "Write this: How blessed are the dead, that is, those who die in the Lord from now on!" "Yes," says the Spirit. "Let them rest from their labors, for their actions follow them."

Jer 25:15 (NIV) This is what the LORD, the God of Israel, said to me: "Take from my hand this cup filled with the wine of my wrath and make all the nations to whom I send you drink it."

The third angel warns people that if they worship the beast (the Antichrist) or his image, or if they receive his mark on their bodies, they too will experience God's wrath. Those who worship the beast are also worshiping Satan. That is the choice everyone will be forced to make: throw in your lot with Christ or with Satan. Refusing to worship the Antichrist won't be easy. The whole world will follow him, and those who refuse will be out on a limb. No one will be able to buy or sell anything without the mark of the beast on their hand or forehead.

The image of the Antichrist will be able to speak, and it will order the executions of those who don't worship it. The saints will endure and be faithful.

The alternative is to be tormented in hell in the presence of the Messiah and his angels after the last judgment (Rev 20:15). This divine punishment is eternal (Rev 20:10). The language may be symbolic, but the torment is real. Jesus speaks about the dangers of hell more than anyone else (Matt 18:8); it is not a doctrine that can be watered down.

The saints are here given clear warning. They are aptly described as people who obey God's commands and believe and trust in Jesus. If they undergo martyrdom, they will be blessed. It is not a shame, or even a disaster. They will be relieved of their sufferings, and they will be rewarded, as Jesus promised the overcomers in each of the churches in chapters 2–3. They will be rewarded for their devotion and service for Christ over the years. Salvation is a gift, but believers will be rewarded for what they have done. Paul's advice is that we should always give ourselves fully to the work of the Lord, because our labor in the Lord is not in vain (1 Cor 15:58).

> Only one life, 'twill soon be past,
> only what's done for Christ will last.

Judgment: Salvation for the Righteous, Destruction for the Wicked

(Rev 14:14–20 ISV)

Then I looked, and there was a white cloud! On the cloud sat someone who was like the Son of Man, with a gold victor's crown on his head and a sharp sickle in his hand. Another angel came out of the Temple, crying out in a loud voice to the one who sat on the cloud, "Swing your sickle, and gather the harvest, for the hour has come to gather it, because the harvest of the earth is fully ripe." The one who sat on the cloud swung his sickle across the earth, and the earth was harvested. Then another angel came out of the Temple in heaven. He, too, had a sharp sickle. From the altar came another angel who had authority over fire. He called out in a loud voice to the angel who had the sharp sickle, "Swing your sharp sickle, and gather the bunches of grapes from the vine of the earth, because those grapes are ripe." So the angel swung his sickle in the earth, gathered the grapes from the earth, and threw them into the great winepress of God's wrath. The wine press was trampled outside the city, and blood flowed from the wine press as high as a horse's bridle for about 1,600 stadia.

Dan 7:13 (NIV) In my vision at night I looked, and there before me was one like a son of man, coming with the clouds of heaven.

Joel 3:12–13 (NIV) Let the nations be roused; let them advance into the Valley of Jehoshaphat, for there I will sit to judge all the nations on every side. Swing the sickle for the harvest is ripe. Come trample the grapes, for the winepress is full and the vats overflow – so great is their wickedness.

The destiny of those on earth is now depicted as two harvests which occur when the Messiah returns. The first one is a grain harvest, which is carried out by the Messiah. The second is a grape harvest, carried out by two angels, one with a sharp sickle and another who has authority over fire (hell). Jesus receives instructions from God via an angel who comes from the temple in heaven. Then he harvests the grain, which symbolizes the saints of all nations. The Son of Man passage in Daniel 7 is about the Messiah and the saints receiving the kingdom and reigning forever. Alluding to that, Jesus said that the nations would see the Son of Man coming on the clouds of the sky, with power and great glory. He would send his angels with a loud trumpet call, and they would gather his elect from all over the world (Matt 24:30b–31). Their destination is not mentioned, but the saints of the Most High will receive the kingdom and possess it forever (Dan 7:18).

In contrast, the angel who has charge of the fire instructs the angel with the sharp sickle to gather the clusters of grapes from the earth's vine, because they are ripe. The angel swings his sickle, gathers its grapes, and throws them into the winepress of God's wrath. This harvest does not refer to the final judgment day, but to the slaughter of the wicked at the battle of Armageddon at Jesus' return. In chapter 19, which portrays Jesus as returning on a white horse, he strikes down the nations and treads the winepress of the fury of the wrath of God Almighty (Rev 19:15). The bloodshed occurs outside Jerusalem, where according to Zechariah 14:2 the nations are gathered to fight. John sees the blood flowing for 184 miles, the length of Israel, to the height of a horse's bridle. This is what John sees in his vision; it is not literal, but the slaughter of the rebellious armies will be enormous. John the Baptist spoke about the Messiah separating the wheat from the chaff (Matt 3:13).

God's Wrath and Praise
from the Overcomers

(Rev 15:1–4 ISV)

I saw another sign in heaven. It was both spectacular and amazing. There were seven angels with the seven last plagues, with which God's wrath is completed. Then I saw what looked like a sea of glass mixed with fire. Those who had conquered the beast, its image, and the number of its name were standing on the sea of glass holding God's harps in their hands. They sang the song of God's servant Moses and the song of the lamb: "Your deeds are both spectacular and amazing, Lord God Almighty. Your ways are just and true, King of the nations. Lord, who won't fear and praise your name? For you alone are holy, and all the nations will come and worship you because your judgments have been revealed."

Lev 26:21 (NIV) If you remain hostile toward me and refuse to listen to me, I will multiply your afflictions seven times over, as your sins deserve.

Ps 86:9 (NIV) All the nations you have made will come and worship before you Lord; they will bring glory to your name.

Isa 66:23 (NIV) From one New Moon to another and from one Sabbath to another, all mankind will come and bow down before me, says the LORD.

Chapters 15–18 describe the punishment meted out by God on the Antichrist, the evil empire called "Babylon", and on rebellious unrepentant mankind who follow the Antichrist. It is depicted in a symbolic way as seven bowls of wrath which are poured out on the earth. These angels and their plagues are called a sign, because they are a portent or foreboding of calamitous events that will happen in the last days. A plague in the Greek language is a blow, or a stroke; figuratively, a blow of fate, or a calamity. These calamities are the final expression of God's anger and retribution to satisfy his justice. They fall specifically on the Antichrist's kingdom and his followers who have thrown in their lot with him. Chapter 16 will reveal the extent of these judgments, including the death of every living thing in the sea, intense heat from the sun scorching people, darkness over the Antichrist's kingdom, and the battle of Armageddon.

Before the calamities arrive, John sees the overcomers, those who were victorious over the Antichrist, standing in heaven beside the sea of glass, a calm glassy sea mixed with fire, before the throne of God. They have harps to praise God. They are happy. They sing the song of Moses (Exod 15), which celebrates victory over an evil empire, which is also the song of the Lamb, who is responsible for their salvation. The title Lord God Almighty applies to both Father and Son; both are universally worshiped. God said everyone will bow before him and everyone will swear by him (Isa 45:23), and Paul said that at the name of Jesus everyone will bow, and everyone will confess that he is Lord (Phil 2:10–11) It is during the time of the messianic kingdom that follows, that survivors of all the nations will come and worship the Father and his anointed Son.

Angels Given Seven Bowls of God's Wrath

(Rev 15:5–8 ISV)

> After these things, I looked, and the Temple, which is the Tent of Testimony in heaven, was open! The seven angels with the seven plagues came out of the Temple wearing clean, shining linen with gold sashes around their chests. One of the four living creatures gave to the seven angels seven gold bowls full of the wrath of God, who lives forever and ever. The Temple was filled with smoke from the glory of God and his power, and no one could enter the Temple until the seven plagues of the seven angels came to an end.
>
> **Exod 32:15** (NIV) Moses turned and went down the mountain with the two tablets of the covenant law in his hands.
>
> **Exod 40:34–35** (NIV) Then the cloud covered the tent of meeting, and the glory of the LORD filled the tabernacle. Moses could not enter the tent of meeting because the cloud had settled on it, and the glory of the LORD filled the tabernacle.

What is about to happen on earth is first determined by God in heaven. God is pictured in his temple, which is here called the tabernacle of the Testimony, or the tent of Meeting that was constructed by the Israelites in the wilderness after the exodus from Egypt. A temple is a place to meet God and the tabernacle was a tent that was portable and the place where Moses met with God. The stone tablets on which were written the ten commandments were placed in the ark of the covenant (a wooden box) in the tabernacle. The word Testimony means a divine charge or code of law and refers to the ten commandments, God's moral law. God's wrath results from his unalterable opposition to sin; the breaking of his commandments. Because of their stubbornness and unrepentant hearts, the bulk of mankind who have rejected these commands will experience the day of God's wrath when his righteous judgment will be revealed (Rom 2:5).

The angels are dressed in white, symbolizing righteous retribution, with gold sashes around their chests, like the dress of the Son of Man (Rev 1:13). The shallow bowls they are given were made of gold and were used for libations. In this symbolic way of expressing things, the bowls are filled with the wrath of the eternal God. The temple will be filled with smoke or cloud, representing the power and glory of God. He is the all-powerful, absolute ruler. Nobody can enter his presence to intercede for the world. God has been patient, but now it is time for him to act. The coming judgments are inevitable; nothing can stop them.

Bowls of Wrath Poured Out on the Earth, the Sea, the Rivers, and the Sun

(Rev 16:1–9 ISV)

Then I heard a loud voice from the Temple saying to the seven angels, "Go and pour the seven bowls of God's wrath on the earth." So the first angel went and poured his bowl on the earth. A horrible, painful sore appeared on the people who had the mark of the beast and worshipped the image. The second angel poured his bowl into the sea. It became like the blood of a dead body, and every living thing in the sea died. The third angel poured his bowl into the rivers and the springs of water, and they turned into blood. Then I heard the angel in charge of the water say, "You are just. You are the one who is and who was, the Holy One, because you have judged these things. You have given them blood to drink because they spilled the blood of saints and prophets. This is what they deserve." Then I heard the altar reply, "Yes, Lord God Almighty, your judgments are true and just." The fourth angel poured his bowl on the sun, which then was allowed to burn people with fire, and they were burned by the fierce heat. They cursed the name of God, who has the authority over these plagues. They did not repent and give him glory.

Ps 79:6–7 (NIV) Pour out your wrath on the nations that do not acknowledge you, on the kingdoms that do not call on your name, for they have devoured Jacob and devastated his homeland.

Ps 78:44 (NIV) He turned their river into blood, they could not drink from their streams.

These catastrophes that come upon the earth correspond to those of the seals and the trumpets. They result from warfare, and here the effect on creation is stressed. More severe than the plagues sent upon Egypt in the book of Exodus, these four bowls affect the whole world. They affect different parts of the environment: the land, the sea, the rivers, and the sun. They are directed toward those who have the mark of the beast and who worship his image, which is just about everyone. After the pouring out of the first bowl, they suffer from foul, painful ulcers, which can be compared to the festering boils inflicted on the Egyptians (Exod 9:8–12). One wonders whether there are any saints left on earth at this time. Jesus asked whether he will find faith on the earth when he comes (Luke 18:8). For the rapture to happen, there must be some.

The second catastrophe hits the oceans, presumably all the oceans, as none is specified. They turn to thick blood and every living thing in the oceans dies. This could be an algal problem rather than literal blood, but the result is devastating, every living thing in the sea dies.

The third catastrophe hits the fresh water rivers and streams, turning them to blood. It is seen as a just punishment, because the wicked inhabitants of the world have shed the blood of saints and prophets, and God has given them blood to drink. God is not unpredictable or capricious; these acts are an expression of his eternal justice and righteousness.

The fourth catastrophe causes the sun to become hotter and scorch people, who in turn curse God who is seen as inflicting this punishment on them. No one repents or glorifies God. The martyrs under the altar in the heavenly temple confirm that God's judgments are right and well-deserved.

The Antichrist's Kingdom Plunged into Darkness as the Kings Gather at Armageddon

(Rev 16:10–16 ISV)

The fifth angel poured his bowl on the throne of the beast. Its kingdom was plunged into darkness. People gnawed on their tongues in anguish and cursed the God of heaven because of their pain-filled sores. But they did not repent of their behavior. The sixth angel poured his bowl on the great Euphrates River. Its water was dried up to prepare the way for the kings from the east. Then I saw three disgusting spirits like frogs come out of the mouth of the dragon, out of the mouth of the beast, and out of the mouth of the false prophet. They are demonic spirits that perform signs. They go to the kings of the whole earth and gather them for the war of the great Day of God Almighty. "See, I am coming like a thief. How blessed is the person who remains alert and keeps his clothes on! He won't have to go naked and let others see his shame." The spirits gathered the kings to the place that is called Armageddon in Hebrew.

Isa 11:15 (NIV) The Lord will dry up the gulf of the Egyptian sea; with a scorching wind he will sweep his hand over the Euphrates River. He will break it up into seven streams so that anyone can cross over in sandals.

Zeph 3:8 (NIV) "Therefore wait for me," declares the Lord, "for the day I will stand up to testify. I have decided to assemble the nations, to gather the kingdoms and to pour out my wrath on them – all my fierce anger. The whole world will be consumed, by the fire of my jealous anger."

Satan gave the Antichrist his power and his throne, but now his throne and kingdom, which seemed so invincible, have been plunged into darkness. The sun was darkened after the sounding of the fourth (Rev 8:12) and fifth (Rev 9:2) trumpets, and in the latter passage, unbelievers suffered the agony of something like scorpion stings. Now after this fifth catastrophe, they continue to curse God and refuse to repent. The darkness may refer to internal strife, because the Antichrist's kingdom will not remain united, meaning that it will be an unstable coalition of nations (Dan 2:43).

The sixth catastrophe is the battle of Armageddon, which is referred to again in Revelation 17:14, 19:19. This is one of the greatest days in the history of our planet; it is the battle of the great day of God Almighty. This battle involves the armies of nations from all over the earth. The Euphrates River was mentioned, when the sixth trumpet was blown (Rev 9:13–16), and two-hundred million mounted troops were released to kill one third of mankind with plagues of fire, smoke and sulfur. Modern warfare will involve nuclear weapons of mass destruction.

In his vision John saw demons that looked like frogs emanating from Satan, the Antichrist, and the false prophet and going to the leaders of the world's nations, where they perform miracles to deceive them into gathering their armies for the battle of Armageddon on the great day of God Almighty.

Verse 15 is significant. The speaker is Jesus, who has not spoken since Revelation 4:1, and he doesn't speak again until Revelation 22:7. But we must keep in mind that the whole book is a revelation from him. He will come unexpectedly, like a thief, but Christians are not caught unawares, and they are clothed in the righteousness that faith in him provides.

The world leaders and their armies will gather in Israel. But who will fight who in this battle? Why will nations from the whole world gather there? Satan is the direct cause. He was cast down from heaven, and in great anger he will try and prevent the Messiah from reigning.

The prophets Jeremiah, Ezekiel and Zechariah say a lot about this battle, but they don't answer all our questions. The Antichrist will set up an image in the temple which is still in Jewish hands. He has authority over all nations, but his kingdom is unstable.

Zechariah tells us that the Lord will gather all nations to Jerusalem to fight against it. The city will be captured, the houses ransacked, and the women raped (Zech 14:2). Daniel 11:40–45 gives us details about the Antichrist waging war against his political enemies. The southern king (an Egyptian coalition) will engage him in battle, and then the northern king (Gog) will storm out against him with chariots (tanks), cavalry and a great fleet of ships. The battle then moves into Israel. Reports from the east (Asia) and the north (Russia) will alarm him, and he sets out to annihilate many, but he meets his end at the beautiful holy mountain (Jerusalem).

When the Lord touches down on the Mount of Olives, the whole earth will quake, and he will go out and defeat those nations. All the holy angels and resurrected saints will be with him (Zech 14:3–5, 2 Thess 1:7, Rev 17:14, 19:14).

The Messiah will be king over the whole earth (Zech 14:9). Zechariah also tells us that the survivors from all the nations that have attacked Jerusalem will go up year after year to worship the King, the Lord Almighty (Zech 14:16). They and their descendants will be the subjects during the millennium, while the saints will constitute the royal family who will rule with the Messiah.

A Severe Earthquake Causes the Cities of the Nations to Collapse

(Rev 16:17–21 ISV)

> The seventh angel threw the contents of his bowl across the sky. A loud voice came from the throne in the Temple and said, "It has happened!" There were flashes of lightning, noises, peals of thunder, and a powerful earthquake. There has never been such a powerful earthquake since people have been on the earth. The great city was split into three parts, and the cities of the nations fell. God remembered to give Babylon the Great the cup of wine filled with the fury of his wrath. Every island vanished, and the mountains could no longer be found. Huge hailstones, each weighing about a talent, fell from the sky on people, who cursed God because the plague of hail was so terrible.
>
> **Ezek 38:20b** (NIV) All the people on the face of the earth will tremble at my presence. The mountains will be overturned, the cliffs will crumble, and every wall will fall to the ground.
>
> **Dan 12:1** (NIV) There will be a time of distress such as has not happened from the beginning of nations until then.
>
> **Matt 24:21** (NIV) For then there will be great distress, unequaled from the beginning of the world until now – and never to be equaled again.

The pouring out of the seventh bowl signals the final great catastrophe that is inflicted on the world. It has already been described at the opening of the sixth seal where there was a great earthquake, cosmic disturbances and the disappearance of every mountain and island (Rev

117

6:12–16). Earthquakes will be felt worldwide. The cities of the nations will collapse; their populations decimated. The angel pours his bowl of God's wrath into the air, because it is from the air that this destruction comes. "It is done", expresses the fact that the Messiah's visitation in judgment on the world is now finished.

The great city that splits into three parts is the great city that rules over the kings of the earth (Rev 17:18). In other words, the leading city of the Antichrist's empire, which is symbolically referred to as Rome and Babylon. Chapter 17 shows these cities of the world to be civilization that has deliberately rejected the will of God, and chapter 18 describes their destruction. The apostle Peter says that the day of the Lord will come like a thief. The heavens will disappear with a roar; the elements will be destroyed by fire, and the earth and everything in it will be laid bare (2 Pet 3:10). And he says that day will bring about the destruction of the heavens by fire, and the elements will melt in the heat. But in keeping with God's promise we are looking forward to a new heaven and a new earth, the home of righteousness (2 Pet 3:12–13). Islands vanishing and mountains not being able to be found indicates they will no longer be recognizable as those that were previously known.

The inhabitants of the world, who are now past repentance, can only curse God. This is the end of God's judgment on the world. The next two chapters describe the great city and its downfall in more detail, and that is followed by yet another description of the coming of the Messiah.

A GREAT PROSTITUTE SITS ON A SCARLET BEAST

(REV 17:1–6 ISV)

Then one of the seven angels who held the seven bowls came and told me, "Come, I will show you how the notorious prostitute who sits on many waters will be judged. The kings of the earth committed sexual immorality with her, and those living on earth became drunk with the wine of her immorality." Then the angel carried me away in the Spirit into a wilderness. I saw a woman sitting on a scarlet beast that was controlled by blasphemy. It had seven heads and ten horns. The woman wore purple and scarlet clothes and was adorned with gold, gems, and pearls. In her hand she was holding a gold cup filled with detestable things and the impurities of her immorality. On her forehead was written a secret name:

BABYLON THE GREAT,
THE MOTHER OF PROSTITUTES
AND DETESTABLE THINGS OF THE EARTH

I saw that the woman was drunk with the blood of the saints and the blood of the witnesses to Jesus. I was very surprised when I saw her.

Gen 11:4, 9a (NIV) Then they said, "Come, let us build ourselves a city, with a tower that reaches to the heavens, so that we may make a name for ourselves; otherwise we will be scattered over the face of the whole earth." … it was called Babel.

Jer 51:7 (NIV) Babylon was a gold cup in the LORD's hand; she made the whole earth drunk. The nations drank her wine; therefore they have now gone mad.

This chapter is about Rome, that city which in the first century had dominion over the kings of the earth. Rome was built on seven hills. She is called Babylon the Great, because she symbolizes all centers of empire which are inevitably characterized by opulence, pride, greed, corruption and the persecution of God's people. The final world empire under the Antichrist will be centered on a great city, and it will have control over all nations; the population of the whole world. The city is called a prostitute, because of her inhabitants' desire for vice and self-gratification.

Genesis 11 records the building of the tower of Babel, which symbolized the pride of man in wanting to make a name for himself. God confused their language; the building was stopped, and the population dispersed. In recent decades a reversal has taken place. Half the world's population now live in urban areas. All global population growth between 2017 and 2030 will be absorbed by cities. The largest cities, Delhi and Tokyo, are approaching forty million each. Global cities are being increasingly linked together through telecommunications, industry, trade, banking, education and politics. That is why we see the woman riding on the beast. The Antichrist will rule the final empire which will include all the great cities of the world.

Since 2008 the tallest building has been the Burj Khalifa in Dubai, standing at 828 meters with 163 floors. There are over fifty buildings higher than 350 meters, half of them in China, and there are many more under construction, including the one-kilometer high Jeddah tower in Saudi Arabia, which is planned for completion in 2020. We may think that these building are marvelous feats of engineering, but God sees them as symbols of man's pride and arrogance. All the cities of the world and their majestic towers will collapse when the angel pours out the seventh bowl of God's wrath.

The prostitute symbolizes these cities, all the mega-cities of the world, and especially the capital city of the Antichrist's empire. The angel told John to come and he would show him the punishment of the great prostitute who sits on many waters; peoples, multitudes, nations and languages. Not only Rome, but all the cities of the world. The fall of Babylon is God's punishment on the cities of the world.

The inhabitants of the world are intoxicated by city life; "the wine of her adulteries". They are attracted by universities, jobs, entertainment, sporting facilities, casinos, hotels and restaurants; but especially the opportunity to make money and get rich. Regarded as necessities of modern life, these facilities lead to greed, materialism, the love of the world, and godlessness.

The woman sits on a scarlet beast covered with blasphemous names. The beast is the empire of the Antichrist that arose from the sea in chapter 13. It is covered in blasphemous names because it is the deification of secular authority. When civil authorities don't acknowledge their role as a service to God, they become proud and arrogant and see themselves as the ultimate authority. They see no value in the spiritual, and spurred on by an atheistic, evolutionistic ideology, they oppose God and the people of God. They are obsessed with the economy and embrace anything that will make money.

City mentality is intoxicated with wealth, symbolized by expensive clothes and jewels. The inhabitants desire freedom from all restraint. They turn their backs on God and his law. The woman is described as drunk with the blood of the saints, the blood of those who bear testimony to Jesus. Rome was known for its persecution of Christians who refused to deny their Lord and worship the emperor. The government of the Antichrist will follow that example.

The Kingdom of the Antichrist

(Rev 17:7–11 ISV)

> "Why are you surprised?" The angel asked me. "I will tell you the secret of the woman and the beast with the seven heads and the ten horns that carries her. The beast that you saw existed once, but is no longer, and is going to crawl out of the bottomless pit and then proceed to its destruction. Those living on earth, whose names were not written in the Book of Life from the foundation of the world, will be surprised when they see the beast because it was, is no longer, and will come again. This calls for a mind that has wisdom. The seven heads are seven mountains on which the woman is sitting. They are also seven kings. Five of them have fallen, one is living, and the other has not yet come. When he comes, he must remain in power for a little while. The beast that was and is no longer is the eighth king, but it belongs with the seven kings and goes to its destruction.

The angel explains the mystery of the woman (Rev 17:18) and the beast she rides. The beast which once was (the Roman empire), now is not (it ceased to exist), and which will come up from the underworld (as a revived world empire) will finally go to its destruction.

It pretends to be like God, who was, who is and who is to come, and like the Lamb who was crucified, came back to life, and is alive forevermore. This time the world empire will have ten horns; a confederation of states, or even a global government. The whole world will be astonished and support this globalization, because it once was (Rome), there was a time when it didn't exist, and now it is back. One of the beast's heads (the Antichrist) had a fatal wound, but the wound was healed

(Rev 13:3). The saints will have discernment and won't follow him, or worship him, or take his mark on their bodies.

The seven heads are described as the seven hills on which Rome was built, but they also represent seven kings. These rulers are different from the confederation of national leaders (the ten horns). Some interpret them as Roman emperors, others as emperors of Egypt, Assyria, Babylonia, Persia, Greece, Rome (then present), and the eighth one, the Antichrist, the emperor of a revived Rome.

The angel said that the beast is an eighth king. He belongs to the seven, but is not one of them, and is going to his destruction. The beast that once was may be a reference to Antiochus Epiphanes 165 B.C., of whom Daniel spoke (Dan 11:21–32), and who is a type of the future Antichrist. Antiochus set up a statue of Zeus in God's temple, called the abomination that causes desolation. Jesus warned that one day people would see another abomination that causes desolation standing in the holy place, and that they should flee. It will be a time of great distress, unequalled from the beginning of the world until then – and never to be equaled again.

World Rulers Surrender Their Power to the Antichrist

(Rev 17:12–18 ISV)

> The ten horns that you saw are ten kings who have not yet received a kingdom. They will receive authority to rule as kings with the beast for one hour. They have one purpose: to give their power and authority to the beast. They will wage war against the lamb, but the lamb will conquer them because he is Lord of lords and King of kings. Those who are called, chosen, and faithful are with him." The angel also told me, "The bodies of water you saw, on which the prostitute is sitting, are peoples, multitudes, nations, and languages. The ten horns and the beast you saw will hate the prostitute. They will leave her abandoned and naked. They will eat her flesh and burn her up with fire, for God has placed within them a desire to carry out his purpose by uniting to give their kingdom to the beast until God's words are fulfilled. The woman you saw is the great city that rules over the kings of the earth."

The ten kings, who represent the global leaders (Rev 16:14), will for a short time, maybe seven years, share authority with the Antichrist. They will make war on the Lamb (the Messiah) by opposing and killing Christians, and by invading Jerusalem and God's temple.

However, when the Messiah returns, he will conquer them, and with him will be his resurrected saints, his called, chosen, and faithful followers. Jesus told his disciples, that they did not choose him; *he chose them* and appointed them to go and bear fruit (John 15:16).

Paul said that God is the blessed and only Ruler, the King of kings and Lord of Lords (1 Tim 6:15). Here in Revelation 17:14 it is the Messiah who is King of kings and Lord of lords. The early church believed in the full deity of Christ.

The Antichrist and the global leaders will hate the prostitute! What can that mean? The terminology comes from Ezekiel 23:25–30 where the downfall of Samaria and Jerusalem is told in allegory about two sisters who were destroyed by the bad alliances they had made. The complex relationship between the leaders of the final world empire and their cities will disintegrate, resulting in civul war.

We know from Daniel 2:41–42 that this final world kingdom will be a divided kingdom. The toes of iron mixed with clay symbolize instability. The nations will not remain united. After the pouring out of the seventh bowl the great city will split into three parts, and the cities of the nations will collapse, presumably due to the great earthquake, but civil war is also a possible cause.

Daniel 11:40–45 says southern and northern confederations will turn against the Antichrist, and storm out against him with chariots and cavalry and a great fleet of ships. The Antichrist will then set out in a great rage to destroy and annihilate many but will come to his end in Israel. Cities will be destroyed in the process, as described in chapter 18. It is God who caused the world leaders to make this bad decision of giving their power and authority to the satanically inspired beast, to accomplish his will (Rev 17:17).

The Fall of Babylon

(Rev 18:1–5 ISV)

After these things, I saw another angel coming down from heaven. He had great authority, and the earth was made bright by his splendor. He cried out in a powerful voice, "Fallen! Babylon the Great has fallen! She has become a home for demons. She is a prison for every unclean spirit, a prison for every unclean bird, and a prison for every unclean and hated beast. For all the nations have drunk from the wine of her sexual immorality, and the kings of the earth have committed sexual immorality with her. The world's businesses have become rich from her luxurious excesses." Then I heard another voice from heaven saying, "Come out of her, my people, so that you don't participate in her sins and also suffer from her diseases. For her sins are piled as high as heaven, and God has remembered her crimes.

Jer 51:37, 45 (NIV) Babylon will be a heap of ruins, a haunt of jackals, an object of horror and scorn, a place where no one lives. ... Come out of her. My people! Run for your lives! Run from the fierce anger of the Lord.

A mighty angel announces the fall of Babylon, the symbol of worldly glory, and the high point of satanic influence. The vocabulary of desolation comes from the prophets. All the nations have been intoxicated by the self-gratification of city life, and the worship of money which is idolatry. The politicians and billionaires benefitted from her commerce, through corrupt dealings with the wealth of her banks, trade and share markets. Babylon stands for the political, commercial and banking systems of the world, centered in all the big cities of the world.

They will never be rebuilt. Like a scene from the Matrix, they will become a haunt for demons and unclean birds. The riches and splendor of the cities will vanish forever, never to be recovered (Rev 18:14).

Christians are advised to leave the city and the evil system that it embodies. We should be yoked together with unbelievers. Righteousness and wickedness have nothing in common. Light and darkness can't have fellowship. There is no agreement between Christ and Satan, and a believer has nothing in common with an unbeliever. So, we should be separate and not touch unclean things (2 Cor 6:14–15, 17).

The last generation of believers is advised to leave the cities of the Antichrist's empire, so that they might escape the calamities which will be poured out on the cities, to punish the inhabitants for their sins, as described in Revelation 16:21 – 18:24.

JUDGMENT ON CORRUPT WORLD COMMERCE

(REV 18:6–10 ISV)

Do to her as she herself has done, and give her double for her deeds. Mix a double drink for her in the cup she mixed. Just as she glorified herself and lived in luxury, inflict on her just as much torture and misery. In her heart she says, 'I am a queen on a throne, not a widow. I will never see misery.' For this reason, her diseases that result in death, misery, and famine will come in a single day. She will be burned up in a fire, because powerful is the Lord God who judges her." The kings of the earth, who committed sexual immorality with her and lived in luxury with her, will cry and mourn over her when they see the smoke rising from the fire that consumes her. Frightened by the torture that she experiences, they will stand far away and cry out, "How terrible, how terrible it is for that great city, the powerful city Babylon, because your judgment arrived in a single hour!"

Ps 137:8 (NIV) Daughter Babylon, doomed to destruction, happy is the one who repays you according to what you have done to us. Happy is the one who seizes your infants and dashes them against the rocks.

Isa 47:7a, 8b, 9 (NIV) You said, "I am forever – the eternal queen!" … I will never be a widow or suffer the loss of children. Both of these will overtake you in a moment, on a single day: loss of children and widowhood. They will come upon you in full measure, in spite of your many sorceries and all your potent spells.

Jer 50:29 (NIV) Summon archers against Babylon, all those who draw the bow. Encamp all around her; let no one escape. Repay her for her deeds; do to her as she has done. For she has defied the LORD, the Holy One of Israel.

Babylon is to be paid back double for her sins, for her pride, for her extravagance, and for murder of prophets and saints and all unjust killings. Her doom will occur in one day, as she is consumed by earthquakes, hail, bombs, missiles and fire.

In verse 7 Babylon boasts that her soldiers are always victorious, they never die on the battlefield. But now she will experience death, mourning, famine and total destruction.

When the world leaders who shared in her wealth see her destruction, they will be horrified and terrified and mourn over her doom. Political leaders, merchants and seamen will all mourn for her.

Isaiah's prophecy against Babylon (Isa 47) is primarily concerned with its defeat by Darius the Med, in 539 BC, but he also foresaw the fall of the final great empire of Babylon (Isa 13). The global extent of the prophecy in the following verses suggest that it refers to the final great Day of the Lord Almighty. This final battle takes on universal proportions as the nations of the world mass together. It is a time of great destruction on earth and few will survive

Read Isaiah's prophecy of the fall of Babylon in Isaiah 13:4–13. It relates to the Babylon that fell in 539 BC as well as the final world empire.

The Collapse of the World Economy

(Rev 18:11–24 ISV)

The world's businesses cry and mourn over her, because no one buys their cargo anymore— cargo of gold, silver, gems, pearls, fine linen, purple cloth, silk, scarlet cloth, all kinds of scented wood, all articles made of ivory, all articles made of very costly wood, bronze, iron, marble, cinnamon, spice, incense, myrrh, frankincense, wine, olive oil, flour, wheat, cattle, sheep, horses, chariots, and slaves (that is, human souls)— "The fruit that you crafted has abandoned you. All your dainties and your splendor are lost, and no one will ever find them again." Frightened by the severity of her punishment, businesses that had become rich because of her will stand at a distance, crying and mourning: "How terrible, how terrible it is for the great city that was clothed in fine linen, purple, and scarlet and was adorned with gold, gems, and pearls, because all this wealth has been destroyed in a single hour!" Every ship's captain, everyone who traveled by ship, sailors, and everyone who made a living from the sea stood far away. When they saw the smoke rising from the fire that consumed her, they began to cry out, "What city was like that great city?" Then they threw dust on their heads and shouted while crying and mourning: "How terrible, how terrible it is for the great city, where all who had ships at sea became rich from her wealth, because it has been destroyed in a single hour! Be happy about her, heaven, saints, apostles, and prophets, for God has condemned her for you!" Then a powerful angel picked up a stone that was like a large millstone and threw it into the sea, saying, "The great city Babylon will be thrown down violently— and will never be found again. The sound of harpists, musicians, flutists, and trumpeters will never be heard within you again. No artisan of any trade will ever be found within you again. The sound of a millstone will never be heard within you again. The light from a lamp will never shine within you again. The voice of a bridegroom and bride will never be heard within you again. For your merchants were the important people of the world, and all the nations were deceived by your witchcraft. The blood of the world's prophets, saints, and all who had been murdered was found within her."

Traders and businessmen can only stand far off and feel terror at the sight of the destruction of the world's great cities. All the great cities will be linked together in the great empire symbolically called "Babylon". The world's great businessmen will mourn because they can't carry on as they had before. The whole world will be in a state of destruction and ruin. It will be up to the Messiah to rebuild the world, and he may do that without cities. The lament is based on Ezekiel's lament of Tyre in Ezekiel 27, where the inventory of imports is similar.

With the end of the city, world trade has come to an end; the ports function no more. All those involved in trade and commerce will mourn the loss of the great cities. Industry is finished, the banks and stock markets are gone, the shopping malls are destroyed. Gone are the casinos and nightclubs. A significant item of trade is the bodies and souls of men.

But the saints will rejoice, as they do in the Hallelujah chorus in Handel's Messiah. That great song of praise is in response to the fall of Babylon. The great cities will be destroyed forever (Rev 19:3). There will be no more music there, no tradesmen, no light, no marriage. Babylon is especially condemned for her sorceries and the death of God's people: saints and prophets and all the innocent people who have been killed on earth.

In chapter 6 when the fifth seal was opened, the martyrs were crying out to God for vengeance. They were then told to wait a little longer until the number of their fellow servants and brothers was complete (Rev 6:11). The prayers of all the saints are offered up on the altar before God's throne (Rev 8:3–4). They are prayers for God's will to be done, prayers for justice and judgment on their persecutors, and prayers for the Messiah's kingdom to come. Now they are told to rejoice (Rev 18:20), because God has judged the evil empire for the way she treated them. The Messiah is about to make his glorious appearance and the saints will be glorified in him and he in them.

Part 3

CHAPTERS 19 – 22

THE MESSIAH'S ARRIVAL AND REIGN

The Hallelujah Chorus

(Rev 19:1–6 ISV)

> After these things, I heard what sounded like the loud voice of a large crowd in heaven, saying, "Hallelujah! Salvation, glory, and power belong to our God. His judgments are true and just. He has condemned the notorious prostitute who corrupted the world with her immorality. He has taken revenge on her for the blood of his servants." A second time they said, "Hallelujah! The smoke goes up from her forever and ever." The twenty-four elders and the four living creatures bowed down and worshipped God, who was sitting on the throne. They said, "Amen! Hallelujah!" A voice came from the throne, saying, "Praise our God, all who serve and fear him, from the least important to the most important." Then I heard what sounded like the voice of a large crowd, like the sound of raging waters, and like the sound of powerful thunderclaps, saying, "Hallelujah! The Lord our God, the Almighty, is reigning.

This chapter is the only one in the New Testament where you will find the word "hallelujah", literally, praise the Lord! The hosts of heaven sing hallelujah because the great city, the center of world empire, has been destroyed, together with all her evil: corruption, greed, vice, crime, robberies, murders, prostitution, drugs, slavery, oppression, blasphemy and the rejection of God's word. City life can be rough, but in the days of the Antichrist it will be many times worse. We read that there was war in heaven (Rev 12:7–12), resulting in Satan being hurled down to earth, and his angels with him. This will mean trouble for the earth and sea, because the devil has come down.

However, the hallelujahs ring out, not only for the punishments and vengeance taken on the great city, but because of the fact that the Lord God Almighty reigns. In Revelation 11:15 it was anticipated that the kingdom of the world would become the kingdom of the Lord and of his Christ, and that he would reign forever. We have now arrived at the most exciting part of the book of Revelation, the last four chapters, which describe the return of the Lord Jesus Christ to this earth to reign. This is our great hope for ourselves and for our planet. It will be a time of restoration, and the saints will reign with Christ in justice and righteousness.

The Trinity is a compact unity of Father, Son and Holy Spirit. When it says, "our Lord God Almighty reigns", we think about the Father, because it is he who is usually referred to as the Almighty, and he is the sovereign Ruler over heaven and earth. But here it refers to Jesus. John hasn't seen a vision of Jesus returning yet, but the hallelujahs announce the immanent beginning of the messianic reign on earth; the kingdom of God that Jesus spoke about so often during his ministry. But before he starts his reign, there is another matter to attend to.

The Wedding Supper
of the Messiah

(Rev 19:7–10 ISV)

"Let us rejoice, be glad, and give him glory, because the marriage of the lamb has come and his bride has made herself ready. She has been given the privilege of wearing fine linen, dazzling and pure." (The fine linen represents the righteous deeds of the saints.) Then the angel told me, "Write this: 'How blessed are those who are invited to the marriage supper of the lamb!'" He also told me, "These are the true words of God." I bowed down at his feet to worship him, but he told me, "Don't do that! I am a fellow servant with you and with your brothers who rely on what Jesus is saying. Worship God, because what Jesus is saying is the spirit of prophecy!"

Isa 54:5 (NIV) For your Maker is your husband – the LORD Almighty is his name – the Holy One of Israel is your Redeemer, he is called the God of all the earth.

Isa 62:5 (NIV) As a young man marries a young woman, so will your Builder marry you; as a bridegroom rejoices over his bride, so will your God rejoice over you.

Hos 2:19–20 (NIV) I will betroth you to me forever; I will betroth you in righteousness and justice, in love and compassion. I will betroth you in faithfulness, and you will acknowledge the LORD.

The wedding of the Lamb has come. Read the parable of the wedding banquet in Matthew 22:1–14. There, Jesus says the kingdom of God is like a king who prepares a wedding banquet for his son. The king is God, the son is Jesus, and the bride is the church, the elect, the righteous, the saints; all those who have accepted the invitation during their lifetimes on earth. This is a cosmic event; it involves both heaven and earth.

In Paul's teaching on marriage, he commands husbands to love their wives, just as Christ loved the church and gave himself up for her (Eph 5:25–27). Christ has purified us by his shed blood, and he has united us to himself in love. We are already betrothed to him, but at his return, there is a wedding, whereby he formally binds us to himself for eternity. There are different metaphors which explain our relationship with God; we are children of God, and we are Christ's brothers, but the marriage union is the closest of them all, because, as Paul said, the two will become one flesh. Paul spoke of a profound mystery, the union of Christ and the church (Eph 5:31b–32). Metaphors of course are not to be taken literally; they guide our imagination. Know that we will never be separated, whatever Christ does, we will be there doing it with him.

As for the bride, she has prepared herself in bright, white linen which contrasts with the purple and scarlet attire of the prostitute. It has a different symbolism to the white robes of those who come out of the Great Tribulation. Those robes are white because they are washed in the blood of the Lamb. Here the white linen stands for the righteous acts of the saints, acts which God prepared in advance for them to do (Eph 2:10). We are not given any details of the marriage ceremony; there are too many things happening at once. But we do have a detailed symbolic description of the New Jerusalem (Rev 21:2 – 22:5); a truly divine community where God and man are united forever.

The Messiah Arrives to Defeat the Nations

(Rev 19:11–16 ISV)

Then I saw heaven standing open, and there was a white horse! Its rider is named Faithful and True. He administers justice and wages war righteously. His eyes are like a flame of fire, and on his head are many royal crowns. He has a name written on him that nobody knows except himself. He is dressed in a robe dipped in blood, and his name is called the Word of God. The armies of heaven, wearing fine linen, white and pure, follow him on white horses. A sharp sword comes out of his mouth to strike down the nations. He will rule them with an iron rod and tread the winepress of the fury of the wrath of God Almighty. On his robe that covers his thigh he has a name written:

KING OF KINGS AND LORD OF LORDS

Exod 15:3 (NIV) The LORD is a warrior.

Ps 2:9 (NIV) You will break them with a rod of iron; you will dash them to pieces like pottery.

Isa 63:2–3 (NIV) Why are your garments red, like those of one treading the winepress? "I have trodden the winepress alone; from the nations no one was with me. I trampled them in my anger and trod them down in my wrath; their blood spattered my garments, and I stained all my clothing."

Isa 66:15–16 (NIV) See, the LORD is coming with fire, and his chariots are like a whirlwind; he will bring down his anger with fury, and his rebuke with flames of fire. For with fire and with his sword the LORD will execute judgment upon all people, and many will be those slain by the LORD.

John 1:1 (NIV) In the beginning was the Word, and the Word was with God, and the Word was God.

Heaven is open. God is intervening dramatically in the history of the world. The Lord Jesus is descending down to earth; not on a literal white horse, but as conqueror, and as the awaited Messiah. He is the way, the truth and the life, and he is ever faithful. He is a warrior, and he will defeat his enemies. Paul used a different metaphor in 2 Thessalonians 1:7b–9, but it is the same occasion. He says the Lord Jesus will be revealed from heaven in blazing fire with his powerful angels. He will punish those who don't know God with everlasting destruction. They will be shut out from the presence of the Lord and from the majesty of his power. The slaughter of men here is not a metaphor (Isa 66:15–16). He will tread the winepress alone; not even the US will support him.

God is a just God, and what Jesus does when he returns is done in strict justice, and in accordance with what is right. His blazing eyes symbolize judgment, while the many crowns express the universality of his royal status. The name written on him, which is known only to himself, may be compared to the white stone with a new name written on it, which Jesus will give to the overcomers. The names will be known only to those who receive them (Rev 2:17).

Jesus' robe is dipped in blood. He is coming to be King of kings and Lord of lords, and the blood spattered on his robe doesn't speak here of his blood shed on the cross; it is symbolic of his victory over his enemies as portrayed in Isaiah 63:1–6 and Revelation 14:14–20. He is treading the winepress of the fury of the wrath of God. The sharp sword coming out of his mouth is a metaphor. There is no sword; it is symbolic of the dynamic word of God which he speaks, and which always accomplishes what is expressed (Heb 4:12). Jesus will only need to say the word and his enemies will be defeated. Similarly, the rod of iron with which he will rule the nations expresses his severe rule.

The armies of heaven will follow him. Apart from the saints who have just been resurrected, there are the mighty angels (2 Thess 1:7). They ride white horses, because they are conquerors, and they wear fine linen, because they are his called, chosen and faithful followers (Rev 17:14,

19:8). They are made righteous through their faith in the blood of Christ, and their mission is righteous and just. Both angels and saints are included, when our Lord Jesus comes with all his holy ones (1 Thess 3:13).

The resurrection of the righteous dead and the rapture of the living saints takes place simultaneously with Jesus' descent from heaven. The rapture isn't explicitly referred to, but is inferred (Rev 14:15–16, cf. Matt 3:12). It is everywhere assumed that the saints pass through the Great Tribulation and are the objects of the Antichrist's persecution (Dan 7:25, Rev 12:17, 13:7). They are counselled to endure and be faithful (Rev 13:10, 14:12).

Jesus said that when he comes, he will send his angels with a loud trumpet call to gather his elect from one end of the earth to another (Matt 24:30–31). Paul adds that when the trumpet sounds, the dead will be raised imperishable and the living will be changed (1 Cor 15:52). The dead in Christ will rise first, then those who are alive will be caught up together with them in the air, and they will be with the Lord forever (1 Thess 4:16b–17).

In Acts 1:11 angels told Jesus' disciples that Jesus will come back in the same way they had seen him go into heaven. Then Zechariah tells us the exact place to which Jesus will come back; his feet will stand on the Mount of Olives, east of Jerusalem (Zech 14:4), the same place from where he ascended. He will reign from Mount Zion. It all happens on the day of the Lord.

THE NATIONS DEFEATED AT ARMAGEDDON

(REV 19:17–21 ISV)

Then I saw an angel standing in the sun. He cried out in a loud voice to all the birds flying overhead, "Come! Gather for the great supper of God. Eat the flesh of kings, the flesh of commanders, the flesh of warriors, the flesh of horses and their riders, and the flesh of all people, both free and slaves, both unimportant and important." Then I saw the beast, the kings of the earth, and their armies gathered to wage war against the rider on the horse and his army. The beast was captured, along with the false prophet who had performed signs on its behalf. By these signs the false prophet had deceived those who had received the mark of the beast and worshipped its image. Both of them were thrown alive into the lake of fire that burns with sulfur. The rest were killed by the sword that belonged to the rider on the horse and that came from his mouth, and all the birds gorged themselves with their flesh.

Ezek 39:17–18a, 20, 22, 29 (NIV) Son of man, this is what the Sovereign LORD says: Call out to every kind of bird and all the wild animals: Assemble and come together from all around to the sacrifice I am preparing for you, the great sacrifice on the mountains of Israel. There you will eat flesh and drink blood. You will eat the flesh of mighty men and drink the blood of the princes of the earth as if they were rams and lambs, goats and bulls. ... At my table you will eat your fill of horses and riders, mighty men and soldiers of every kind ... From that day forward the house of Israel will know that I am the LORD their God. ... I will pour out my Spirit on the people of Israel."

Dan 7:11 (NIV) Then I continued to watch because of the boastful words the horn was speaking. I kept looking until the beast was slain, and its body destroyed and thrown into the blazing fire.

This great supper of God is in stark contrast to the wedding feast of the Lamb. The great supper of God is a metaphor which fires the imagination to consider the fate of the armies of the world who thought they could foil the purposes of God and his Messiah. After doing their best to rid the world of Christianity, they will come from all over the world to capture the city of God, Jerusalem, the capital city of God's chosen people Israel. Why do the nations conspire, and the peoples plot in vain, asks the Psalmist? Why do the earth's leaders take their stand against the Lord and against his Messiah? (Ps 2:1–2). Joel says the Lord will roar from Zion and thunder from Jerusalem, the earth and the sky will tremble, and the Lord will be a refuge for his people Israel (Joel 3:16).

Zechariah says that the Lord will strike all the nations that fight against Jerusalem with a plague. Their flesh will rot while they are still standing, their eyes will rot in their sockets, and their tongues will rot in their mouths. They will be stricken by the Lord with such panic that they will attack each other (Zech 14:12–13).

The Antichrist, the leaders of the earth, and their armies will gather to fight against Israel at the symbolical battlefield called Armageddon (Rev 16:16). They don't realize that they will fight against the omnipotent Jesus and his army. This is a great historical event which will happen in Israel. A battle between the nations of the world, who have come to capture Jerusalem, and the Jewish nation which is defending their capital city.

The Lord said it is he who will gather all the nations to Jerusalem to fight against it. Then after the city is captured, the houses ransacked, and the women raped, he will go out and fight against those nations. His feet will stand on the Mount of Olives (Zech 14:2–4) as he returns to Jerusalem.

The Antichrist will be captured, along with the false prophet, and they will be thrown alive into the fiery lake of burning sulfur, a metaphor for hell, the place of final torment. The kings and their armies will be killed by the judicial verdict which comes from the mouth of Jesus. The vultures will eat their dead corpses. This is literal. This may be the meaning of Jesus' word that where the corpse is, there the vultures will gather, but this proverb is simply telling them to look for the obvious signs.

The identity of the place called Armageddon is not clear. Megiddo was a town about sixty miles NW of Jerusalem, and the nearby plain was an ancient battleground. The armies that will come against Jerusalem for the battle of Armageddon are described in Ezekiel 38–39 as Gog and Magog, but this battle should not be confused with the final act of rebellion described in Revelation 20:8–9, which is also attributed to Gog and Magog. The latter follows the millennium, but there is no actual battle. Those armies will be destroyed by fire from heaven, followed by Satan being cast into hell, the final judgment, and the end of the world.

The battle of Armageddon and associated events are the final acts of God's judgment on an unbelieving world. This passage should be compared with the opening of the sixth seal (Rev 6:12–17), the pouring out of the seventh bowl (Rev 16:17–21) and the description given in Ezekiel 38:18–23. A great earthquake will devastate all creation. Mountains will crumble, walls will collapse, and rain, hailstones and burning sulfur will fall on the troops. The vultures are called to feast on the dead. Ezekiel emphasizes the conversion of Israel at this time. He said that they will then know that the Lord is their God, and that the Lord will no longer hide his face from them; rather, he will pour out his Spirit on them (Ezek 39:28–29).

Satan Imprisoned for a Thousand Years

(Rev 20:1–3 ISV)

Then I saw an angel coming down from heaven, holding the key to the bottomless pit, with a large chain in his hand. He captured the dragon, that ancient serpent, also known as the devil and Satan, and tied him up for a thousand years. He threw him into the bottomless pit, locked it, and sealed it over him to keep him from deceiving the nations anymore until the thousand years were over. After that, he must be set free for a little while.

Isa 24:21–23 (NIV) In that day the LORD will punish the powers in the heavens above and the kings on the earth below. They will be herded together like prisoners bound in a dungeon; they will be shut up in prison and be punished after many days. The moon will be dismayed, the sun ashamed; for the LORD Almighty will reign on Mount Zion and in Jerusalem, and before its elders – with great glory.

The vision that John saw following the vision of Armageddon is that of Satan being captured and bound for a thousand years (the millennium). The Antichrist and the false prophet will be captured and cast immediately into hell (Rev 19:20), but Satan will be bound and imprisoned in the Abyss for the duration of Messiah's reign on earth.

There is no reason to regard the thousand years as figurative. It may be approximate, but we cannot say that the period is more or less. The revelation that Jesus and the saints will rule on earth for a thousand years is a central eschatological teaching which influences everything else, including the two resurrections, the two judgments, and the glorious future of Israel and Jerusalem.

Satan will be securely imprisoned in the Abyss by an angel. The word "abyss" originally meant the unseen depths of the sea, or the bottomless pit, then the underworld. The reference here is not to a literal part of our physical creation, it is a spiritual underworld, the abode of demons and a place of torment (Luke 8:31).

The mention of a chain, Satan being bound, and the locking and sealing of the pit, all emphasize the fact that Satan will have no influence on earth during the time of his incarceration. There is no way he can deceive the nations or do anything during that time; not until he is released for a short time at the end. Satan has already been identified as the enormous red dragon of chapter 13. He is that ancient serpent (Gen 3:1) called the devil, who leads the whole world astray.

Many people in Africa and other parts of the world deal with evil spirits on a daily basis. Some people sacrifice to spirits and seek their help. Some are possessed by them, while others suffer sickness inflicted by black magic and sorcery. I have seen Muslims seek refuge in the churches because Christians are mostly immune from demonic activity, and the pastors' prayers are effective. Victims often testify to having been *bound* by spirits. A leg or arm or mouth may be *bound*. Local practitioners can *bind* a spirit so that it can no longer harm a victim. Jesus' teaching on binding and losing is very relevant for these people.

After Satan's incarceration, it is in God's plan that he be released for a short time. In his infinite, and sometimes mysterious wisdom, God tolerates evil and uses it to his glory, but one day he will eliminate evil completely from the universe.

The Resurrection of the Righteous

(Rev 20:4–6 ISV)

Then I saw thrones, and those who sat on them were given authority to judge. I also saw the souls of those who had been beheaded because of their testimony about Jesus and because of the word of God. They had not worshipped the beast or its image and had not received its mark on their foreheads or hands. They came back to life and ruled with the Messiah for a thousand years. The rest of the dead did not come back to life until the thousand years were over. This is the first resurrection. How blessed and holy are those who participate in the first resurrection! The second death has no power over them. They will be priests of God and the Messiah, and will rule with him for a thousand years.

Dan 7:9 (NIV) As I looked, thrones were set in place, and the Ancient of days took his seat.

Luke 14:14 (NIV) Although they cannot repay you, you will be repaid at the resurrection of the righteous.

According to Daniel 2:34, 44 the eternal kingdom of God is built on the ruins of the sinful empires of the world. Only after the statue that represents these kingdoms is smashed does the rock that smashed them become a huge mountain and fill the earth. When the final kingdom is destroyed and Satan is bound (cf. Matt 12:29), the Messiah will be free to restore the fallen world, where justice, righteousness and the knowledge of the Lord will abound.

John saw thrones on which were seated those who had been given authority to judge. We saw these thrones in chapter 4. Those seated there are representatives of the saints from both Israel and the church. It is the redeemed who are the children of God who will judge and rule with the Messiah. Jesus told his disciples that at the renewal of everything, when the he sits on his glorious throne, they would also sit on twelve thrones, judging the twelve tribes of Israel (Matt 19:28). When Zechariah spoke about the Lord's future rule from Jerusalem, he said many nations would be joined to him and become his people (Zech 2:10–13). He will again choose Jerusalem and will live there.

Then John saw the souls of those who had been martyred during the Great Tribulation. They had not worshiped the Antichrist. He had seen their souls before (Rev 6:9), but this time he sees them come back to life and reign with Christ for a thousand years. We are then told that this is the first resurrection. Jesus spoke about the *resurrection of the righteous* (Luke 14:14, 20:35–36), where he speaks of those who are considered worthy of taking part in that age (the millennium) and in the resurrection *from* the dead.

Paul said that when Jesus comes, *those who belong to him* will be resurrected (1 Cor 15:23), *and the dead in Christ* will rise first (1 Thess 4:16). They precede those who are still alive in Christ. The point is, the resurrection of unbelievers is never mentioned in connection with Christ's coming. When he comes, he sends his angels to gather the elect (Matt 24:31). Two will be in one bed; one will be taken and the other left. Two will be grinding grain together; one will be taken and the other left (Luke 17:34–35).

John very clearly states that there are two resurrections, by adding that the rest of the dead are not resurrected until the thousand years of messianic reign are over. It is not only the martyrs who are resurrected, it is the whole church who will reign with Christ (Rev 5:9), including those who are raptured (1 Thess 4:17). The church is blessed and holy because they take part in the first resurrection and will be priests of God and of Christ during the millennium. This is the clear and simple interpretation of these verses.

Satan's Release and the Final Rebellion

(Rev 20:7–10 ISV)

When the thousand years are over, Satan will be freed from his prison. He will go out to deceive Gog and Magog, the nations at the four corners of the earth, and gather them for war. They are as numerous as the sands of the seashore. They marched over the broad expanse of the earth and surrounded the camp of the saints and the beloved city. Fire came from God out of heaven and burned them up, and the devil who deceived them was thrown into the lake of fire and sulfur, where the beast and the false prophet were. They will be tortured day and night forever and ever.

Ezek 38:2–6 (NIV) Son of man, set your face against Gog, of the land of Magog, the chief prince of Meshech and Tubal; prophesy against him and say: "This is what the Sovereign LORD says: I am against you. Gog, chief prince of Meshech and Tubal. I will turn you around, put hooks in your jaws and bring you out with your whole army – your horses, your horsemen fully armed, and a great horde with large and small shields, all of them brandishing their swords. Persia (Iran), Cush (Sudan), and Put (Libya) will be with them, all with shields and helmets, also Gomer with all its troops, and Beth Togarmah from the far north with all its troops – the many nations with you."

The "four corners of the earth" is an idiom meaning everywhere on earth, with emphasis on far-off places. Verse 8 refers to Gog and Magog (Ezek 38–39) who symbolize remote hostile nations who come to attack Israel both before and after the millennium.

It seems extraordinary that Satan could deceive the nations once more, after they have experienced a thousand-year peaceful and prosperous reign under the Messiah. We have no evidence that the subjects of the messianic kingdom will be born again of God's Spirit, apart from the conversion of Israel, which will be a special act of God's grace, when the Messiah defeats their enemies at Armageddon. This final act of Satan may occur to illustrate how callous is the unregenerate heart of man. They gather for battle and travel across the face of the earth and surround the camp of the saints. The center of Messiah's kingdom on earth will be Jerusalem and the nation of Israel, his people. Israel's habitation during their wanderings after the exodus was always called their camp.

There is no battle. Satan and his armies come to a swift end when fire comes down from heaven and devours them. The devil is cast into hell where the Antichrist and the false prophet were thrown, and where they will be tormented day and night forever. A necessary and just sentence. The subjects of the messianic kingdom enter it as unbelievers, survivors of the tribulation period (Zech 14:18). They will marry and have children and live long lives (Isa 65:20). The world will be divided into nations and ethnic groups, and they will be punished if they don't go to Jerusalem regularly to worship the Messiah. The earth will be full of the knowledge of the Lord as the waters cover the sea (Isa 11:9).

Jesus will be King over all the earth, and the saints, who were resurrected at Jesus' return, will be ruling with him. The sovereignty, power and greatness of the kingdoms under the whole heaven will be handed over to them, the people of the Most High (Dan 7:27). As a resurrected, immortal people, they will live in the New Jerusalem, described in Revelation 21:2 – 22:5. It symbolizes a glorified mode of existence in union with Christ, the church being depicted as the wife of the Lamb. The glory of this city will be seen above earthly Jerusalem, but the inhabitants will be in another space-time dimension.

Judgment Day and the End of the World

(Rev 20:11–15 ISV)

> Then I saw a large, white throne and the one who was sitting on it. The earth and the heavens fled from his presence, and no place was found for them. I saw the dead, both unimportant and important, standing in front of the throne, and books were open. Another book was opened—the Book of Life. The dead were judged according to their actions, as recorded in the books. The sea gave up the dead that were in it, and Death and Hades gave up the dead that were in them, and all were judged according to their actions. Death and Hades were thrown into the lake of fire. (This is the second death—the lake of fire.) Anyone whose name was not found written in the Book of Life was thrown into the lake of fire.
>
> **Dan 7:10** (NIV) The court was seated, and the books were opened.

The great white throne is not mentioned elsewhere in the Bible; it is symbolic of God's sovereign authority and justice. The one depicted as sitting on the throne is of course God, who is not defined as the Son or the Father. But Jesus said that the Father judges no one, all judgment has been entrusted to him (John 5:22). And in the parable of the Sheep and the Goats, it is the Messiah who sits on his throne in heavenly glory to judge people (Matt 25:31).

On judgment day, the earth and sky will flee from God's presence, and no place will be found for them. Some think this signals the end of this present earth and sky, others think this is poetic imagery expressing the fear of the corruptible in the presence of God. This vision of the last judgment has a sense of finality about it. Jesus declared that heaven and earth would pass away, but his words would never pass away (Matt 5:18, 24:35). Hebrews 12:27 says that what can be shaken – created things – will be removed, so that only what cannot be shaken may remain.

John sees the unregenerate dead, now resurrected, whether they were important or not (Rev 20:5). He also sees the book of life, that was mentioned earlier (Rev 3:5, 13:8,17:8). The dead cannot complain about their judgment; everyone will be judged according to what they have done. The Lord searches the heart and examines the mind, to reward a man according to his conduct and what his deeds deserve (Jer 17:10). The righteous are also rewarded for their deeds (Matt 16:27), but that occurred at the first resurrection, at Jesus' coming, so that they might enjoy their rewards during the millennium. The opening of books is not literal; we are to realize that everything we have said and done is accurately recorded in the mind of God. Nothing has been missed, and he will reward those who deserve rewarding, and punish those who deserve punishment.

Death and Hades are thrown into hellfire, but again, this is a metaphor. You can't throw things like death and Hades into a fire. The significance is that they are finally annihilated. But, unfortunately, there are millions of unbelievers who will be cast into hell to be tormented day and night forever (Rev 20:10). Even if it is not literal fire, the torment will be real. They are "outside", with no access to the tree of life, or to the Holy City.

A New Heaven and a New Earth

(Rev 21:1 ISV)

> Then I saw a new heaven and a new earth, because the first heaven and the first earth had disappeared, and the sea was gone.
>
> **Isa 65:17–18** (NIV) See, I will create new heavens and a new earth. The former things will not be remembered, nor will they come to mind. But be glad and rejoice forever in what I will create, for I will create Jerusalem to be a delight and its people a joy. I will rejoice over Jerusalem and take delight in my people; the sound of weeping and of crying will be heard in it no more.
>
> **Isa 66:22–23** (NIV) As the new heavens and the new earth that I make will endure before me, declares the LORD, so will your name and descendants endure. From one New Moon to another and from one Sabbath to another, all mankind will come and bow down before me, says the LORD.

Revelation 21:1 does not describe a newly created earth. The word "new" often describes something that is repaired or renewed. John says in verse 4 that it is the old order of things that has passed away. The earth will not pass away until the last judgment.

The expression "a new heaven and new earth" alludes to the Isaiah passages, and on reading them, it is clear that Isaiah is referring to a renewal of the present earth, not a new planet. What John sees here is the thousand-year reign that he mentioned six times in Revelation 20:4–6. It is the "renewal of all things" or "regeneration" spoken of by Jesus (Matt 19:28), the liberation of the creation from its bondage to decay spoken of by Paul (Rom 8:18–21). The elect will receive a kingdom (kingship) that cannot be shaken (Heb 12:28). The sky and the earth will be shaken, so that a transformation of the world will take place, making way for the kingdom of the Messiah.

John doesn't only see a new earth; he sees a new sky as well. He builds on a prophecy by Haggai which predicts that God will shake the sky, the earth, the sea, the dry land and the nations. The condition of the whole of the visible creation will be overturned and reduced to ruins. The time is during the Great Tribulation, when the nations will be defeated, their armies destroyed, and all the accomplishments of ungodly civilizations over the millennia will be removed. Then the treasure (or the desired one), of all nations, will come and the temple will be filled with glory (Hag 2:6). The treasure is the gold and precious stones which will be brought to Jerusalem to adorn the earthly temple. The desired one would be the Messiah who is desired and longed for by Christians in all the nations of the world.

John's millennial earth has no sea. If this is taken literally, it means a complete change in the meteorology of the new earth. The amount of water would remain constant but be distributed in a different way, so that destructive weather patterns would cease. The lifting of the Edenic curse will bring about many changes in the new world. But the evidence is in favor of the sea being a symbol of chaos and the turbulent, rebellious nations (Dan 7:2–3, Rev 12:17, 13:1) which will certainly be subdued during the millennium. Messiah's rule will extend from sea to sea (Zech 9:10) and on judgment day, after the millennium, the sea gives up its dead (Rev 20:13), indicating that there will still be oceans during the millennium.

The rest of the chapter is a symbolic description of the New Jerusalem, which should not be taken as a description of the new earth.

The New Jerusalem

(Rev 21:2–8 ISV)

I also saw the holy city, New Jerusalem, coming down from God out of heaven, prepared like a bride adorned for her husband. I heard a loud voice from the throne say, "See, the tent of God is among humans! He will make his home with them, and they will be his people. God himself will be with them, and he will be their God. He will wipe every tear from their eyes. There won't be death anymore. There won't be any grief, crying, or pain, because the first things have disappeared." The one sitting on the throne said, "See, I am making all things new!" He said, "Write this: 'These words are trustworthy and true.'" Then he told me, "It has happened! I am the Alpha and the Omega, the beginning and the end. I will freely give a drink from the spring of the water of life to the one who is thirsty. The person who conquers will inherit these things. I will be his God, and he will be my son. But people who are cowardly, unfaithful, detestable, murderers, sexually immoral, sorcerers, idolaters, and all liars will find themselves in the lake that burns with fire and sulfur. This is the second death."

Isa 55:1 (NIV) Come, everyone who is thirsty, come to the waters! Also, you that have no money, come, buy, and eat! Come! Buy wine and milk without money and without price.

Abraham was looking forward to a city whose architect and builder is God (Heb 11:10). It is our hope also. We have come to Mount Zion, to the heavenly Jerusalem, the city of the living God (Heb 12:22). This is New Jerusalem, which comes down out of heaven from God. The adjective "heavenly" indicates origin. In Galatians 4:26 Paul calls it the

Jerusalem that is above, or *from* above, a city who is our mother, because we are her inhabitants.

New Jerusalem comes down from heaven (presumably to the earth) at the beginning of the millennium, and God says that he is making all things new (Rev 21:5). The marriage of the Lamb was signaled before (Rev 19:7–9) and now the glorified resurrected church is ready to reign with the Messiah. The city is described metaphorically as a bride beautifully dressed for her husband. Christ is the bridegroom; the saints are the bride. It is not a literal marriage; marriage symbolizes the intimate relationship between Christ and the church, the spiritual union between God and man. God will live with man and be their God, and they will be his people. There will be no more suffering in this new environment; no more death or pain. This is something new. God said he will make everything new.

"It is done", evil is defeated and the saints are victorious. God is the Beginning and the End, time doesn't limit him, everything he has decided is certain. Our minds can't conceive what God has prepared for those who love him, but the invitation is there for all. All one needs is a thirst for God. Jesus said, if anyone is thirsty, he should come to him and drink (John 7:37). The overcomers who do God's will until the end will inherit all God's blessings, but the sinners' lot is in hell. Those who are out to enjoy life, those who fear insult and persecution for Christ's sake, those who turn back, and those who surrender to their baser desires, they will all share in the devil's fate; eternal torment, the second death.

Union with Christ in New Jerusalem

(Rev 21:9–18 ISV)

Then one of the seven angels who had the seven bowls full of the seven last plagues came to me and said, "Come! I will show you the bride, the wife of the lamb." He carried me away in the Spirit to a large, high mountain and showed me the holy city, Jerusalem, coming down from God out of heaven. The glory of God was its radiance, and its light was like a valuable gem, like jasper, as clear as crystal. It had a large, high wall with twelve gates. Twelve angels were at the gates, and the names of the twelve tribes of Israel were written on the gates. There were three gates on the east, three gates on the north, three gates on the south, and three gates on the west. The wall of the city had twelve foundations, and the twelve names of the twelve apostles of the lamb were written on them. The angel who was talking to me had a gold measuring rod to measure the city, its gates, and its walls. The city was cubic in shape: its length was the same as its width. He measured the city with his rod, and it measured at 12,000 stadia: Its length, width, and height were the same. He also measured its wall. According to the human measurement that the angel was using, it was 144 cubits. Its wall was made of jasper. The city was made of pure gold, as clear as glass.

Ezek 40:2, 3b (NIV) In visions of God he took me to the land of Israel and set me on a very high mountain, on whose south side were some buildings that looked like a city ... I saw a man ... with a measuring rod in his hand.

Ezek 48:30–31a (NIV) These will be the exits of the city: Beginning on the north side, which is 4,500 cubits long, the gates of the city will be named after the tribes of Israel.

An angel shows John the bride of the Lamb; that is, the Messiah's wife. But he does not see a woman; he is taken up a very high mountain to watch the descent of a city that is a 1,380–mile cube. This cube of course is a metaphor; we have to imagine what it really means. This is not an earthly city; it descends from heaven, and it shines with the glory of God, like precious jewels. This city represents God's glorified people. Just imagine all those precious jewels, pearls and gold. That symbolizes our ultimate glorification. The community is huge, numbering in the millions, and it is made up of people who have been redeemed from every tribe, nation and language. When the holy city descends to earth, it will shine with the glory of God.

The number twelve recurs throughout. There are twelve gates symbolizing free access, with twelve angels symbolizing security. The gates are inscribed with the names of the twelve tribes of Israel, and there are twelve foundations inscribed with the names of the twelve apostles. The redeemed are God's people from both old and new covenants, from ancient Israel and the church. Each side of the city is twelve-thousand stadia and the walls are 144 (12 x 12) cubits thick! That simply symbolizes the security of the city. The population has previously been symbolized as numbering 144,000 (14:1). Paul said that Christians are no longer foreigners and aliens, but fellow citizens with God's people and members of God's household, built on the foundation of the apostles and prophets, with Christ Jesus himself as the chief cornerstone. In him the whole building is joined together and rises to become a holy temple in the Lord (Eph 2:19–21). Our living conditions are not revealed. No one has seen or heard or conceived what God has prepared for those who love him (1 Cor 2:9). The holy city, the New Jerusalem is a symbolic representation of our life in union with Christ during the millennium, and it is also an appropriate description of our existence into eternity.

The Glory of New Jerusalem

(Rev 21:19–27 ISV)

The foundations of the city wall were decorated with all kinds of gems: The first foundation was jasper, the second sapphire, the third agate, the fourth emerald, the fifth onyx, the sixth carnelian, the seventh chrysolite, the eighth beryl, the ninth topaz, the tenth chrysoprase, the eleventh jacinth and the twelfth amethyst. The twelve gates were twelve pearls, and each gate was made of a single pearl. The street of the city was made of pure gold, as clear as glass. I saw no temple in it, because the Lord God Almighty and the lamb are its temple. The city doesn't need any sun or moon to give it light, because the glory of God gave it light, and the lamb was its lamp. The nations will walk in its light, and the kings of the earth will bring their glory into it. Its gates will never be shut at the end of the day—because there will be no night there. People will bring the glory and wealth of the nations into it. Nothing unclean, or anyone who does anything detestable, and no one who tells lies will ever enter it. Only those whose names are written in the lamb's Book of Life will enter it.

Isa 24:23 (NIV) The moon will be dismayed, the sun ashamed; for the LORD Almighty will reign on Mount Zion and in Jerusalem, and before its elders – with great glory.

Isa 54:11–12 (NIV) Afflicted city, lashed by storms and not comforted, I will build you with stones of turquoise, your foundations with lapus lazuli. I will make your battlements of rubies, your gates of sparkling jewels, and all your walls of precious stones.

Isa 60:3, 5b, 11, 19 (NIV) Nations will come to your light, and kings to the brightness of your dawn ... The wealth on the seas will be brought to you, to you the riches of the nations will come. ... Your gates will always stand open, they will never be shut, day or night ... The sun will no more be your light by day, nor will the brightness of the moon shine on you, for the LORD will be your everlasting light, and your God will be your glory.

The significance of the precious stones is their sparkling brilliance; the reason wealthy women adorn themselves with them. The breastplate of the Jewish high priest also had twelve precious stones. The streets of transparent gold are symbolic of the city's glory. The city does not need light from sun or moon, their light would be eclipsed by the glory of God and the Lamb.

The nations that walk by its light (cf. Isa 2:3) are the subjects of the millennial kingdom who live throughout the world. The earth's leaders will bring their glory to Jerusalem during the millennium, but they cannot enter the New Jerusalem. The relation between the two is not clear. Isaiah saw the glory of Jerusalem in the last days (Isa 60), and the prophets always framed their prophecies in the context of this present world. God says he is making everything new, the old order of doing things will pass away. New Jerusalem will be our millennial home, but it is a metaphor. We don't know much about our future state.

There are over two billion people who claim to be Christians in the world today. Only the Lord knows those who are his, but the complete number of the redeemed from all time may be a billion or more. Where are they going to live when they return to earth with Jesus? The New Jerusalem comes down from heaven to earth, and we may be living in a different dimension from which we will travel to earth as angels do.

Life in Paradise

(Rev 22:1–5 NIV)

Then the angel showed me the river of the water of life, as clear as crystal, flowing from the throne of God and of the Lamb ²down the middle of the great street of the city. On each side of the river stood the tree of life, bearing twelve crops of fruit, yielding its fruit every month. And the leaves of the tree are for the healing of the nations. ³No longer will there be any curse. The throne of God and of the Lamb will be in the city, and his servants will serve him. ⁴They will see his face, and his name will be on their foreheads. ⁵There will be no more night. They will not need the light of a lamp or the light of the sun, for the Lord God will give them light. And they will reign for ever and ever.

Gen 2:9b (NIV) In the middle of the garden were the tree of life and the tree of the knowledge of good and evil.

Ps 46:4 (NIV) There is a river whose streams make glad the city of God, the holy place where the Most High dwells.

Ezek 47:1, 12 (NIV) The man brought me back to the entrance to the temple, and I saw water coming out from under the threshold of the temple toward the east. ... Fruit trees of all kinds will grow on both banks of the river. Their leaves will not wither, nor will their fruit fail. Every month they will bear fruit, because the water from the sanctuary flows to them. Their fruit will serve for food and their leaves for healing.

Zech 14:6–8 (NIV) On that day there will be neither sunlight nor cold, frosty darkness. It will be a unique day – a day known only to the Lord – with no distinction between day and night. When evening comes, there will be light. On that day living water will flow out from Jerusalem, half of it east to the Dead Sea and half of it west to the Mediterranean Sea, in summer and in winter.

Living water in John's gospel is a metaphor for the Holy Spirit. Jesus said the water he gives us becomes a spring of water welling up in us to eternal life (John 4:14). Streams of living water will flow from within the believer – the Holy Spirit whom believers receive from God (John 7:38–39a).

In Ezekiel, water flows from the temple, but in New Jerusalem there is no temple; the water flows from the throne of God and the Lamb down the main street. The tree of life, which was in the garden of Eden, is seen on both sides of this river, and the overcomers will have access to its fruit (Rev 2:7). It symbolizes eternal life communicated by the Holy Spirit; that state in which God and believers are restored to perfect fellowship.

The tree of life produces twelve kinds of fruit, with a fresh crop every month.; another metaphor which should not be taken literally. The tree of life symbolizes the fact that whatever we need to nourish and keep our bodies healthy will be extravagantly provided for. The leaves are for the healing of the nations. The saints don't need medication, but they will be ruling the world and serving God and the Lamb, bringing healing and restoration from their throne to the unregenerate nations outside the gates. The curse our world has experienced since Adam was driven out of the garden of Eden will diminish, but it will not be eliminated as long as unregenerate humanity exists.

There will be no daytime and nighttime in the city; God's glory is its light. Jesus said the pure in heart are blessed, because they will see God (Matt 5:8). After the resurrection we will see God and serve him and reign with him forever. We will be members of the royal family, while the people we will rule over outside are the "dogs" and sorcerers and sexually immoral and murderers and idolaters.

This Teaching is Trustworthy and True

(Rev 22:6–11 NIV)

The angel said to me, "These words are trustworthy and true. The Lord, the God who inspires the prophets, sent his angel to show his servants the things that must soon take place." ⁷"Look, I am coming soon! Blessed is the one who keeps the words of the prophecy in this book." ⁸I, John, am the one who heard and saw these things. And when I had heard and seen them, I fell down to worship at the feet of the angel who had been showing them to me. ⁹But he said to me, "Don't do that! I am a fellow servant with you and with your fellow prophets and with all who keep the words of this scroll. Worship God!" ¹⁰Then he told me, "Do not seal up the words of the prophecy of this scroll, because the time is near. ¹¹Let the one who does wrong continue to do wrong; let the vile person continue to be vile; let the one who does right continue to do right; and let the holy person continue to be holy."

Dan 8:26 (NIV) Seal up the vision, for it concerns the distant future.

Dan 12:10 (NIV) Many will be purified, made spotless and refined, but the wicked will continue to be wicked.

The remaining verses are an epilogue. The angel reassures John that the visions he has seen and the words he has heard are reliable and true. They are the things that must soon take place. The major part of the book of Revelation remains to be fulfilled, as has been explained in this book. It is God who guides the spirits of prophets to prophesy the truth. Jesus himself speaks again (22:7) to reassure us that he is coming soon, without delay. We may find that perplexing, as he said it nearly two-thousand years ago, but he repeats his statement three times in this chapter, as well as previously (Rev 3:11), so he certainly wants us to live in anticipation of his coming. We should be alert. And that is why he has not given us a clearer timetable of what is to come. We are blessed if we pay attention to the prophetic words in this book, and if we stand fast during times of persecution.

This is the second time (cf. Rev 19:10) that John is warned not to worship angels. He was of course overawed by the occasions. God is the only one who warrants our worship, not angels, or political or church leaders.

Daniel was told to seal his prophecy, because it concerned the distant future. John is told *not* to seal his prophecy, because we are living in the last days, and the time is near. People can still find faith through hearing the gospel and being cleansed, they will endeavor to do what is right and be holy, as God is holy. However, there comes a time when repentance and change become impossible, because character has been determined by a lifetime of bad habits. One day a choice will have to be made between Christ and the Antichrist, and once a choice for the Antichrist has been made, the decision will be final. The wrongdoers will continue in their vile behavior and wrongdoing. But today, the invitation is still there to come to Jesus (Rev 22:17).

The Messiah is Coming with His Reward

(Rev 22:12–16 NIV)

Look, I am coming soon! My reward is with me, and I will give to each person according to what they have done. [13]I am the Alpha and the Omega, the First and the Last, the Beginning and the End. [14]Blessed are those who wash their robes, that they may have the right to the tree of life and may go through the gates into the city. [15]Outside are the dogs, those who practice magic arts, the sexually immoral, the murderers, the idolaters and everyone who loves and practices falsehood. [16]I, Jesus, have sent my angel to give you this testimony for the churches. I am the Root and the Offspring of David, and the bright Morning Star.

Num 24:17b (NIV) I see him, but not now; I behold him, but not near. A star will come out of Jacob; a scepter will rise out of Israel.

Ps 62:12 (NIV) You reward everyone according to what they have done.

Isa 62:11b (NIV) See, your Savior comes! See, his reward is with him, and his recompense accompanies him.

Matt 16:27 (NIV) For the Son of Man is going to come in his Father's glory with his angels, and then he will reward each person according to what they have done.

Listen to the words of Jesus, the Messiah. When he comes, there will be rewards for the saints, and punishment for the wicked. God's judgments are fair; each person is treated according to what he has done in this life. In the beatitudes Jesus said that if we are righteous, the kingdom of God will be ours, we will inherit the earth, we will see God, and we will be called the sons of God. Jesus promised those who made good use of the gifts that they were given, that he would put them in charge of many things (Matt 25:21), and that some, at least, would rule over cities (Luke 19:17). Paul said they will be rewarded with eternal life, glory, honor and peace (Rom 2:7, 10). They will be resurrected and be immortal, and they will reign with Christ. They will judge the world and even angels (1 Cor 6:2–3). In addition to general rewards that all the saints will enjoy, Christ will reward each person according to what he or she has done.

In Revelation 1:8, 21:6 a voice says he is the Alpha and Omega, but it could be the Father or the Son speaking. Here it is clearly the Son who claims to be the Beginning and the End. He is God, the Lord of the Old Testament, the Creator and Sustainer of the universe. He is before all things, and in him all things hold together (Col 1:17).

The saints are blessed, because they have been cleansed in the blood of Jesus, giving them access to the tree of life and to the Holy City. The "dogs" are outside. This is a metaphor for the wicked who are outside of salvation. Their place will one day be in the lake that burns with fire and sulfur (Rev 21:8), but here the context is the millennium and "outside" means outside of the holy city. The nations over whom the Messiah and the saints will rule are the wicked who, because of their sin, threw in their lot with the Antichrist.

Jesus sent his angel to pass on this testimony to all believers. It is to be trusted. Jesus is the coming Messiah, the Davidic king. He is the star of David, as seen by Balaam. His coming will herald a new dawn following the dark days of the Great Tribulation.

Let all Come and Receive the Gift of Life

(Rev 22:17–21 NIV)

The Spirit and the bride say, "Come!" And let the one who hears say, "Come!" Let the one who is thirsty come; and let the one who wishes take the free gift of the water of life. [18]I warn everyone who hears the words of the prophecy of this scroll: If anyone adds anything to them, God will add to that person the plagues described in this scroll. [19]And if anyone takes words away from this scroll of prophecy, God will take away from that person any share in the tree of life and in the holy city, which are described in this scroll. [20]He who testifies to these things says, "Yes, I am coming soon." Amen. Come, Lord Jesus. [21]The grace of the Lord Jesus be with God's people. Amen.

Deut 4:2 (NIV) Do not add to what I command you and do not subtract from it, but keep the commands of the LORD your God that I give you.

The book finishes appropriately with an invitation and a warning. The Holy Spirit and the church have always been the ones responsible for drawing people to Christ through the word of God. Those who respond continue the invitation. Salvation is a gift; it can't be earned. As the woman at the well was informed, the water of life is the eternal and supernatural life communicated to us by the Holy Spirit (John 7:38–39). If God's Spirit lives in you, just as God raised Jesus from the dead, he will also raise you from the dead and give life to your mortal bodies (Rom 8:11).

Moses warned the Israelites long ago that they should not add or subtract from God's word. The present warning is given specifically for the book of Revelation. Because it is not an easy book to interpret, there is the temptation to find fault with the text, or to force it into a preconceived mold. This is forbidden; nothing should be added or taken away. The warning is not only addressed to scholars, but to *everyone who hears* the prophecy contained in the book. The consequences are dire.

Jesus says he is coming soon. Our response should be to make sure we know him, and that our sins are forgiven. We should desire and pray for his return, even when life is comfortable. The book closes with a benediction for those who have washed their robes. Let everyone ask themselves if they are clothed in the righteousness of Christ which is obtained through faith alone.

Appendices

The appendices are explanations of symbolism and end-of-age events and personages connected with the book of Revelation. Understanding them will give you a better appreciation of this wonderful revelation and just how the end-of-age events will pan out

1. Symbolism in Revelation

The book of Revelation consists of a series of visions that were communicated to the apostle John by an angel. The visions are like little video clips that illustrate end of world events. The events are real future events that should be interpreted literally, but many words and phrases used in these visions have a symbolic meaning, and those words should not be interpreted literally. The symbolic meaning of the words is often found in the Old Testament. In the following list of symbolic words and phrases, relevant references from the OT and Revelation are given in parentheses.

word or phrase	symbolic meaning
12 (Gen 49:28)	number for God's people (Rev 21:12)
144,000 (12 x 12 x 1000)	number for total church (7:4, 14:1)
24 elders around God's throne	church representatives (4:4) (Israel 12 + church 12)
666	Antichrist's number (13:18) counterfeit trinity (16:13)
7 spirits/lamps (Exod 25:37)	Holy Spirit (1:4, 4:5)
7 (Gen 4:15, 7:2)	completeness
Abyss	underworld, home of evil spirits (9:1, 20:1)
altar (Gen 8:20)	sacrifice (6:9, 16:7) prayer (8:3, 9:13)
ancient serpent (Gen 3:1)	Satan (12:9, 20:2)
Armageddon (2 Kings 23:29)	great battlefield in Israel (16:16)
Babylon the Great (Dan 4:30)	capital of world empire (14:8, 16:19, 17:5, 18:2,10,21)
Balaam's teaching (Num 31:16)	making money through preaching (2:14)

beast (Dan 7:3)

world empire (13:2)

the Antichrist (13:8)

False Prophet (13:11)

blood flowing to horse's bridle

enormous bloodshed (14:20)

book of life (Exod 32:32)

list of names of the redeemed
(3:5, 20:12)

bride (Hos 2:19)

church (19:7)

New Jerusalem (3:12, 21:2, 9)

chain

restrainer (20:1)

crown

royal authority (3:11, 4:4, 6:2,
13:2,14:14,19:12)

crown of life

reward of eternal life (2:10)

desert (Hos 2:14)

place of refuge (12:6, 14)

double-edged/sharp sword
(Isa 49:2)

authority of God's word
(1:16, 2:16, 19:15)

eagle (Ezek 1:10)

representative of birds (4:7)

eagle flying overhead

universal proclamation (8:13)

eagle's wings (Exod 19:4)

divine providence (12:14)

Egypt (Exod 7:13)

stubborn inhabitants of
Jerusalem (11:8)

fiery mountain falls into the sea

nuclear bomb? (8:8)

fire (Isa 66:16, Matt 5:22)

hell (14:18, 20:14)

anger (19:12)

foundations

teaching of the apostles
(21:14)

Gog and Magog (Ezek 38:2)

eschatological enemies from
the north (20:8)

gold

genuine riches/value (3:18,
21:18)

great blazing star

ballistic missile? (8:10)

Hades (Gen 37:35)

home of spirits of the dead,
Hebrew: Sheol (1:18, 20:13)

hail and fire mixed with blood	modern warfare (8:7)
harp	worship instrument (5:8, 14:2, 15:2)
head	king (13:2, 17:3)
horn (Dan 7:24)	leader and his authority (12:3, 13:2, 11, 17:12)
incense (Ps 141:2)	prayer (5:8, 8:3–4)
iron scepter (Ps 2:9)	toughness/strictness (2:27, 12:5, 19:15)
Jezebel (1 Kings 16:31)	false prophetess (2:20)
key of David (Isa 22:22)	key to Messiah's kingdom (3:7)
keys of death and Hades	Jesus' power to redeem (1:18)
Lamb (John 1:29)	1. Christ as sacrificial victim (5:6, 12:11, 13:8) 2. Messiah as victorious military leader (14:1, 17:14)
Lamb's wedding feast (Hos 2:19)	celebration of union with Christ (19:7)
lampstand (Zech 4:2, 11)	local church giving light (1:12, 20) two witnesses (11:4)
leaves of tree of life (Ezek 47:12)	healing for the nations (22:2)
lightning (Exod 19:16)	God's royal decrees (4:5, 8:5, 11:19, 16:18)
linen, bright and clean	righteousness of the saints (15:6, 19:8, 14)
lion (Gen 49:9)	king of Judah (5:5)
lion (Ezek 1:10)	representing wild animals (4:7)

lion's teeth (Joel 1:6) — fierceness (9:8, 17, 13:2)

living creatures (Ezek 1:6) — representatives of creation (4:6, 5:6, 7:11, 14:3)

living water/water of life (Zech 14:8) — life communicated by God's Spirit (7:17, 21:6, 22:1, 17)

locusts (Joel 1:4, 6)) — great army (9:3, 7)

morning star (Num 24:17) — Messiah as harbinger of a new dawn (22:16)

New Jerusalem — glorified church (3:12, 21:2)

one third of the stars — fallen angels? (12:4)

open door (Isa 22:22) — evangelistic access (3:8)

opening the seals — revealing world's destiny (6:1)

ox (Ezek 1:10) — representing domestic animals (4:7)

pale horse (Zech 6:3) — harbinger of death (6:8)

palm branches (Lev 23:40) — celebration (7:9)

precious stones/jewels (Exod 28:15–21) — value, glory (18:12, 21:11, 19)

prostitute (Isa 23:17) — immoral commerce (17:1, 15), immoral attraction of city life (19:2)

rainbow (Gen 9:13) — covenant (4:3, 10:1)

red dragon (Isa 27:1) — Satan (12:3)

rider on black horse (Zech 6:2) — harbinger of hunger (6:5)

rider on red horse (Zech 6:3) — harbinger of war (6:4)

river of the water of life (Ps 46:4) — Holy Spirit (22:1)

river spewed by Satan (Isa 43:2) — wave of persecution or distress (12:15–16)

root of David (Isa 11:1, 10) — Messiah, descendant of David (5:5, 22:16)

scales — food scarcity (6:5)

scroll (little, open) (Ezek 3:1–3)

contents of Rev 12–16) (10:2, 8)

scroll (rolled up) (Ezek 2:9–10)

contents of Rev 6–18 (5:1)

sea (Dan 7:2–3)

rebellious nations (13:1, 20:13, 21:1)

sea becoming blood

"red tide" algae? (16:3–4)

sea of glass (Exod 24:10, Ezek 1:22)

peace at God's throne (4:6, 15:2)

second death

hell (2:11, 20:6, 14, 21:8)

sickle (Joel 3:13)

harvesting tool (14:14, 18)

Sodom (Gen 19)

immoral city (11:8)

star that fell from heaven (Isa 14:12)

Satan or Abaddon (9:1)

stars in Jesus' hand (Gen 1:16b–17)

luminaries, church leaders (1:20)

sun and moon and 12 stars (Gen 37:9)

Jacob and family (12:1)

sword (Isa 3:25)

war (6:4, 13:10)

throne (Isa 6:1)

royal rule (2:13, 3:21, 4:2, 6:16, 7:9, 13:2, 16:10, 20:4, 21:5, 22:5)

thunder (Ps 18:13)

God's voice (4:5, 8:5, 10:3, 11:19, 16:18)

tree of life (Gen 2:9)

source of eternal life (22:2, 14, 19)

tribes of Israel (Gen 29–30)

God's people (7:4, 21:12)

trumpet (1 Sam 13:3)

news announcer (8:2, 10:7, 11:15)

white hair (Dan 7:9)

venerable (1:14)

white horse (Zech 6:3)

harbinger of conquest (6:2, 19:11)

white robe (Rev 3:4)	imputed righteousness (6:11, 7:9)
white throne	final judgment (20:11)
wine (Jer 51:7)	attraction of city life (17:2, 18:3)
winepress (Isa 63:2–3)	God's punishment (14:12, 19:15)
woman's hair	antennae (on tanks)? (9:8)
Zion (Ps 2:6, Isa 24:23)	place of messianic rule (14:1)

2. Sequence of Events during the Great Tribulation

Caveat – the following chronology is a suggestion only. We have been given many details about future end-of-age events, but they are scattered throughout the Bible. Daniel was instructed to shut up the words of prophecy and seal the book until the time of the end, to keep them safe for future generations to read (Dan 12:4). Then, in the book of Revelation, an angel told John that he should not seal up the words of prophecy of his book, because the time is near. Past generations have found it difficult to discern how the future will play out, but as we draw closer to the time of Jesus' return, world events and Bible prophecies will coalesce. This is an effort to put the various end-of-age events in chronological order. The events and the order in which they will occur are still not clear. This attempt to create a sequence of events gives a possible scenario of how the events may be played out.

Preliminary Signs (Matt 24)

1. False prophets and false religions (24:4-5, 11).
2. Wars, famines, and earthquakes (Mat 24:6-7).
3. Christian persecution (Mat 24:9).
4. Increase of evil, rebellion and apostasy (Mat 24:9-10).
5. Israel is regathered in their land (Isa 11:11-12, Jer 30:3, Ezek 11:17, 37:21, Hos 3:4-5, Amos 9:14-15).
6. Gospel preached throughout the world (Mat 24:14).

The First Half of the Final Seven Years

1. Two anointed witnesses (Zech 4:9, 11-14, Rev 11:4-6) preach in Jerusalem for 42 months while a third Jewish temple is built (Mat 24:15, 2 Thess 2:4, Rev 11:2).

2. Before hostilities begin, angels mark God's servants with a seal for their eternal security (Rev 7:1–8).

3. War in heaven! Satan and his demons are thrown down to earth. He is angry, knowing that his time is short (Rev 12:7–12).

4. Satan empowers a final, worldwide, empire, symbolically called Babylon, a renewed form of the Roman empire which will take peace from the world (Dan 7:22-24, Rev 6:2-4, 13:1-4).

5. Worldwide famine, pestilence and death follow the warfare and one quarter of humanity perishes (Rev 6.5–8) and much of the environment is ruined (Rev 8:7–12).

6. Satan tries to destroy Israel by invasion, but the earth (UN?) counteracts it. Just as God bore Israel on eagles' wings and brought them from Egypt to the wilderness of Sinai (Hos 2:14), so he will save them again and care for them for 42 months (Rev 12:13-14).

7. The Antichrist arises (Rev 13:5-6, Dan 11:36-39) and also the false prophet (Rev 13:11-18).

8. When the witnesses finished their testimony, the Antichrist invades Jerusalem and kills them. God brings them back to life, and the Israeli remnant give glory to God (Rev 11:7–13).

The Last Half of the Final Seven Years

1. The nations (Babylon) trample Jerusalem during the last 42 months (Rev 11:2).

2. Empowered by Satan, the Antichrist slanders God and sets himself up in God's place in the temple at Jerusalem (2 Thes 2:4). He exercises his authority over every tribe and nation, demanding worship for 42 months, killing Christians, and annulling their influence (Rev 12:17, 13:5-8).

3. The false prophet deceives the nations with miracles and enforces worship of the Antichrist and requires everyone to receive his mark (666) (Rev 13:11–17, Dan 9:27).

4. Victorious martyrs of all nations wait in heaven (Rev 6:9–11, 7:9–14) for the Messiah's kingdom (Rev 14:1–5, 15:2).

5. The kingdom of the Antichrist is plunged into darkness as a third of humanity is killed by rebellious worldwide armies, symbolically known as Gog (Ezek 38-39) converging on Jerusalem for the battle of Armageddon (Rev 9:13–19, 16:10–16, 19:17–21, Dan 11:44).

6. Unbelievers are tormented for five months by the effects of nuclear, biological and chemical warfare (Rev 9:1–11). They long to die.

7. God's wrath is poured out, producing painful sores on unbelievers, pollution of the sea and fresh water sources, and intensification of the sun's heat (Rev 16:1–9).

3. SEQUENCE OF EVENTS AT AND AFTER THE MESSIAH'S RETURN

1. The Messiah returns on the clouds of heaven with power and great glory (Matt 24:30, Rev 19:11–16).

2. The righteous dead are resurrected and meet the Lord in the air (1 Thess 4:16, Rev 20:4), while living saints are raptured (1 Thess 4:17, Rev 14:14–16).

3. The Messiah continues his descent with his saints to the Mount of Olives (Zech 14:4, 5c) and then to the temple in Jerusalem (Ezek 43:1-4).

4. A great worldwide earthquake (Ezek 38:19–20, Rev 6:12, 11:13, 16:18) causes megacities to collapse (Rev 6:12–17 16:17–21) and the mighty last world empire of Babylon falls (Rev 17–18).

5. The New Jerusalem, the eternal home of God and angels and the redeemed, comes down out of heaven (Rev 21:2 – 22:5). It is in a heavenly dimension, but it's light is seen above earthly Jerusalem (Isa 60:1-3).

6. The Messiah will inflict vengeance on unbelievers (2 Thess 1:7) and empower Israel to destroy the world's armies and kings at Armageddon (Zech 12:2–9, 14:3, Rev 16:16, 19:11–16). The Antichrist and the false prophet will be defeated and cast into hell (2 Thess 2:8, Rev 19:19–20). Satan is bound for 1000 years (Rev 20:1–3).

7. The Lord will pour out his Spirit on Israel (Isa 32:15, Azek 39:29, Joel 2:28, Zech 12:10). Their conversion is too late for them to be included in the kingdom. All Israel will be gathered to their promised land and they will all know the Lord and be known as the Lord's people.

8. Along with Israel, the unbelieving survivors of the Great Tribulation (Zech 14:16) will live normal human lives as subjects of the messianic kingdom), while the resurrected saints

will live in the New Jerusalem and rule over the world with the Messiah for 1000 years (Zech 14:9, Rev 11:15, 20:6).

9.   Heaven and earth are renewed (Isa 65:17-19, Rev 21:1, 5) as the curse is progressively lifted from the world. The animal kingdom will live in harmony with man and the Messiah will rule the nations with a rod of iron with justice and righteousness (Isa 11:4-6).

10. The Messiah's glory will be seen above Jerusalem (Isa 60:1-3) and will fill the temple (Ezek 43 2-4), and all the nations will make yearly pilgrimages to Jerusalem to worship the Lord (Zech 14:16-18). The knowledge of the Lord will fill the earth as the waters cover the sea (Isa 11:9).

11. When the 1000 years are over, Satan will be released and he will instigate a final rebellion of mankind against the holy saints in Jerusalem. Fire will consume them and Satan will be thrown into hell where he will be tormented day and night forever (Rev 20:7–10).

12. The wicked will be judged (Rev 20:11–13, 15), death and Hades will cease to exist (Rev 20:14), and the physical universe will disappear (Rev 20:11). The redeemed of all nations, including Israel, will reign with God forever (Rev 22:3–5).

4. Great Tribulation Events

Revelation 6–18 describes events that will happen during the seven-year tribulation before Jesus the Messiah returns to earth to reign during the millennium. The Great Tribulation is not only a time of war caused by the Antichrist; it will also be a time of great persecution for Christians and Jews and anyone who refuses to worship him. Christians will have to choose whether they are going to honor Christ or the Antichrist. There can be no compromise. Jesus assured his disciples that God will give justice to his elect quickly, but he then asked them whether, when he comes, he will find faith on earth (Luke 18:8).

The Great Tribulation is characterized by the plagues initiated by the apocalyptic horsemen and announced by the seven trumpets, and finished with the pouring out of the seven bowls of God's wrath (Rev 16). These plagues are directed towards unbelievers, and many are the result of the Antichrist's activities. The sea and rivers will be polluted, there will be global warming, and darkness will cover the earth to the extent that the sun is darkened, and the moon becomes red. On top of that, there will be the greatest earthquake known to man that will cause utter desolation and destruction throughout the earth, including the destruction of the world's cities and the disappearance of islands and mountains (Rev 16:18–21).

The Apostasy

Paul said that Jesus would not return until the rebellion occurs first, and the man of lawlessness is revealed (2 Thess 2:3). The first sign will be a rejection of all divine order by the majority of mankind, which will open the way for the man of lawlessness, the Antichrist, to become a world dictator. The apostasy will also affect the church. Paul said that in later times some people will abandon the faith and follow deceiving spirits and things taught by demons (1 Tim 4:1) Jesus prophesied the same thing (Matt 24:10–12), when he said that many will fall away, they will betray one another and hate one another. False prophets will appear and the love of many people will grow cold.

The Final World Empire

The second event is described in Revelation 13:1–4 with the rise of the final world empire, which is called the beast, following the prophet Daniel's terminology of four world empires, and especially this final world empire. This "beast" will devour the whole earth and be terrifying and frightening and very powerful. It will crush and devour its victims and trample underfoot what is left (Dan 7:19). It has ten horns and seven heads. The horns represent leaders who will reign simultaneously, and the heads are seven hills. As Rome was built on seven hills and was the empire of John's day, this final world empire is seen as a revived Roman empire, symbolically called Babylon, a coalition of world countries, a result of globalization. The empire will be satanically empowered, and all men will worship Satan and the empire he has established.

God's Servants are Sealed

The Great Tribulation is so-called because it is a time of distress for everybody, the greatest distress this world has known since Noah's flood, including God's people; Israel and the church. The final world empire will be opposed to the God of the Bible and to all who follow him. In chapter seven angels hold back destructive forces on earth to prevent any destructive activity until the servants of God are sealed. The seal identifies them as belonging to God and protects them from harm. There will be many martyrs, so the seal does not guarantee protection from death, but as Jesus said, his followers would be hated by all because of his name, but not a hair of their heads will perish. The resurrection will be imminent, when the righteous dead will return to life with perfect bodies. The number of those sealed is given as 144,000 from all the tribes of Israel. This is interpreted as being a symbolic number representing all who believe in Jesus.

The World Conquered by the Beast

The first four seals reveal four apocalyptic horsemen; destructive forces that wreak havoc throughout the world. The first one represents conquest, the second warfare, the third famine and the fourth death. No less than twenty-five percent of the world's population will be killed during this time as a result of warfare and resulting famines and epidemics. The first four trumpets describe the same period as the first four seals, but they concentrate on the physical result of the conquest. One third of the land will be burnt, possibly by weapons of modern warfare. One third of sea creatures will be killed and one third of ships will be destroyed by naval battles and nuclear missiles. One third of fresh water sources will be polluted by radiation from the nuclear warfare. One third of the light of the sun and moon will be obscured by the smoke of the warfare, resulting in a frightening semi-darkness. This is all (and enough) that is revealed to us about the first half of the seven-year tribulation period.

The Rise of the Antichrist and the False Prophet

The Antichrist is described as a "mouth" given to the beast, because of his arrogance and slander against God. He will exercise authority for forty-two months (Rev 13:5), which is the second three-and-a-half-year period of the seven-year tribulation. The Antichrist will make war against the saints and conquer them, empowered by Satan. He is described as a "little horn", but he manages to defeat three of the ten world leaders, and then to take control as world dictator. The false prophet exercises all the power of the Antichrist on his behalf and deceives people with signs and miracles. He makes everyone worship the Antichrist and sets up an image of him in a rebuilt temple at Jerusalem, and he makes the image talk. This image was prophesied by Daniel and mentioned by Jesus, who warned those in Judea at that time to flee to the mountains. Worship the Antichrist or die! The false prophet will force everyone to take the mark of the beast, and without it nobody will be able to buy or sell anything.

Satan Hurled down to Earth

The midpoint of the tribulation is marked by a very significant event in heaven. There is war in heaven (Rev 12:7) and Satan and his angels lose their place there. He is hurled down, and the earth and sea are warned that the devil has come down to them and he is filled with fury, because he knows that his time is short (Rev 12:12). His first inclination is to destroy Israel, but God has prepared a place to protect them in the wilderness (12:14–16) for three and a half years. Satan then pursues Christians. *Woe* to the earth and sea, because the devil has come down in great wrath knowing that his time is short. After the fourth trumpet was blown, John saw an eagle flying overhead crying, woe, woe, woe to those who dwell on the earth, because of the remaining three trumpets that were to be blown, announcing escalating judgments on rebellious humanity.

The Martyrs

There will be many martyrs during this time, perhaps most Christians, because the choice will be between Jesus or the Antichrist. At the opening of the fifth seal the martyrs call out to God for vengeance. In chapter 20 they come to life; they are resurrected and reign with Christ. God's servants have been sealed, so their eternal salvation is guaranteed. There are several visions of martyrs in heaven waiting for the Lord's return (Rev 6:9–11, 7:9–17, 14:1–5, 15:1–4). They sing a new song and have God's name written on their foreheads. They wear white robes because they have been made righteous through the blood of Christ.

Final Military Maneuvers

Following the fifth trumpet there is a detailed description of locusts who sting like scorpions. The plague is directed toward unbelievers to torment them for five months. These locusts are portrayed in the book of Joel as destructive agents. They may be crowd-controlling tanks. After the sixth trumpet, armies of two-hundred million from the east are released at the Euphrates River and one third of the world's population is killed by the warfare that follows. They are killed by the plagues of fire, smoke and sulfur which issue from the horses' mouths – presumably gunfire from tanks, shells from mortars, missiles and bombs. The sixth bowl is poured out on the Euphrates and refers to the same event. Evil spirits go forth from the dragon, the beast and the false prophet to gather armies from the whole world to descend on Israel for the battle of Armageddon. The final world empire is unstable, a mixture of iron and clay, a coalition of nations from all over the world. The coalition will unravel, the nations will fight each other, and Jerusalem will be the unfortunate center of attention.

The Antichrist and Jerusalem

Daniel 9:27 tells us that the Antichrist will make a covenant with many for seven years, but in the middle of the "week", he will put an end to sacrifice and offering, and on a wing of the temple, he will set up an abomination that causes desolation. Jesus said that when the Jews in Judea see this abomination standing in the holy place, they should flee to the mountains. Chapter 11 tells us about two witnesses who preach in Jerusalem for three and a half years during the time that the Gentiles trample Jerusalem. It will be in the Antichrist's hands, but the two witnesses are powerful and will continue their witness during this time. The Antichrist eventually kills them, but they come back to life after three and a half days and ascend to heaven. There is a great earthquake, seven thousand die in the city, and the survivors in Jerusalem give glory to God.

God's Wrath Poured Out on an Unbelieving World

After the first bowl, sores break out on people who bear the beast's mark. After the second bowl everything in the sea dies. After the third bowl all fresh water turns to blood and those who shed the blood of saints are left with blood to drink. After the fourth bowl, the sun burns unbelievers. The fifth angel pours out his bowl on the throne of the beast and his kingdom is thrown into darkness resulting in anguish and pain. It may be at this time that the beast hates the prostitute (the great city, maybe all cities) and destroys her. The Antichrist and his confederate of kings deliberately, or accidentally through nuclear war, destroy the financial and commercial system of the world kingdom.

The Fall of Babylon and All the Cities

When the seventh bowl is poured out into the air, a loud voice from God's throne says that it is done. There is a great earthquake, the greatest earthquake ever, presumably the same one mentioned previously (Rev 6:12, 11:13). This results in the fall of Babylon and all the megacities of the world (Rev 16:19, 17:1). Mountains and islands disappear. Huge hailstones fall on men. This final destruction is also described after the sixth seal is opened. There will be a great earthquake, the sun will be darkened, islands & mountains will disappear, and even the most important people will try and hide from God.

5. The Antichrist

The Antichrist will rise to power during this time and he will do as he pleases. He'll exalt and magnify himself above every religion, speaking amazing things against God. He'll succeed until what has been determined by God is carried out. He'll glorify the god of fortresses; military power, including nuclear armaments. He'll recognize those who honor him. He'll invade many countries in great anger, intending to destroy many, moving swiftly and sweeping through, extending his power over many countries, including the beautiful land (Israel). There will be continuous war during his reign.

The prophet Daniel, who lived 2,600 years ago, gives us the most information about the Antichrist (Dan 7–9, 11), although the name Antichrist is not used as a proper name in scripture. Jesus does not name him, Paul calls him the 'man of sin' and 'the lawless one' (2 Thess 2:1–12), while John simply calls him 'the animal' or 'the beast'. Daniel calls him a 'little horn', and 'a despicable person', and said that he had eyes like those of a human being and a mouth that boasted with audacious claims. He watched him as he waged war against the saints and prevailed against them. He will attempt to alter times and laws, which may include the calendar year, religious holidays, and Judeo-Christian morality. He'll succeed for three and a half years until he is killed, and his body is destroyed and burnt in hell. Then the kingdom, authority, and magnificence of all nations of the earth will be given to the saints.

The Antichrist will be remarkably destructive and will destroy mighty men and the holy people. He'll cause deceit to prosper under his leadership. He will most probably arise from Europe, as the Roman emperors did. As his name suggests, he will oppose God and the saints, and God will allow him to conquer them during the three and half years that precede the Messiah's arrival.

The "abomination of desolation", or "the sacrilegious object that causes desecration", spoken about by Jesus (Matt 24:15), is generally believed to be a statue or image of the Antichrist. Jesus referred us to Daniel 9:26–27 to learn about this, showing that the Antichrist would be a last-days' figure. Daniel 9:27 suggests that the Antichrist will make a covenant with Israel for seven years and allow their temple to be rebuilt, then, in the middle of the week, he will break the treaty, suspending both the sacrifice and grain offerings at the temple. and then he will set himself up in the new temple and demand worship from everyone in the world. The final three-and-a-half years will be a time of terrible suffering, worse than any dictatorship that has preceded it. It will be a time of trouble, particularly for Israel (Jer 30:7), but God will rescue them.

Jesus warned future Jews that when they saw this object of desolation, they should flee immediately to the mountains, saying that if God did not shorten those days, no one would survive. This probably means nuclear war, which would continue for the next three and a half years, with Jerusalem as the main center of attention.

Paul was thinking about the Great Tribulation when he counseled the Thessalonians, saying that the Day of the Lord will not come unless the rebellion takes place first and the man of sin, who is destined for destruction, is revealed. He'll oppose and exalt himself above every so-called god and object of worship and seat himself in the temple of God and declare himself to be God (2 Thess 2:3–4).

The apostle John adds more teaching about the Antichrist (Rev13:5–8), saying that he would reign for forty-two months and exalt himself above everyone, including God and his people. God will allow him to make war against the saints and conquer them, resulting in a vast number of martyrdoms. He will have authority over every tribe, people, language and nation and every non-Christian will worship him. He has a false prophet (Rev 13:11–18) who commands his worship and causes everyone to be marked with the name or number (666) of the

Antichrist. Without it no one will be able to buy or sell. The Antichrist and his false prophet will be captured at the battle of Armageddon. Paul said that Jesus will overthrow him with the breath of his mouth and destroy him by the splendor of his coming (2 Thess 2:8) and John adds that they will be thrown alive into the fiery lake of burning sulfur (Rev 19:20).

By demanding universal worship, he will cause the whole world to rebel against God. He will plunge the world into a war so horrific that it slaughters a third of the world's population (Rev 9:18). However, his empire will be unstable. After uprisings from Egypt and Russia, there will be rebellion from the east and the north which can be identified with a two-hundred million strong army released at the Euphrates River (Rev 9:13–16) and culminating in Armageddon at the Lord's return, when the Antichrist will come to his end (Rev 19:20) between the Mediterranean and Dead seas (Dan 11:36–45).

6. Babylon

The last world empire, symbolically called "Babylon", will be a coalition of many, if not all the countries of the world. King Nebuchadnezzar had a dream of a great statue representing four empires, generally interpreted as being Babylonia, Medo-Persia, Greece and Rome. The fourth kingdom is symbolically called Babylon in the book of Revelation. It was the Roman Empire in John's day and will be an extension of that empire in the last days. It is described as being as strong as iron, because it will shatter and crush everything. The feet and toes made partly of clay and partly of iron represent a divided kingdom. It will still have the strength of iron, but the kingdom will be both strong and brittle; it won't remain united. During the time of the final empire, God will set up a kingdom that will never be destroyed. This is the kingdom of God that Jesus proclaimed, his own messianic kingdom. He will shatter and crush all corrupt human rule, and his kingdom will stand forever (Dan 2:40–45).

In Nebuchadnezzar's dream the fourth empire (Rome) was represented by the legs of iron (Dan 2:40), but he also dreamt of details about the feet and toes (Dan 2:41–43), which Daniel interpreted as representing the same empire at a later time and in a different form. The peoples would be mixed through immigration and interracial marriages, as is happening all over the world today, and they won't be truly united.

Then Daniel had a vision of four beasts that represent the same four empires of Nebuchadnezzar's dream. He described the fourth beast as an awe-inspiring, terrifying, and viciously strong animal that would devour the whole earth. It had large, iron teeth, it devoured and crushed things, and then trampled under its feet whatever remained. Different from all the previous animals, it had ten horns. This is the beast described in Revelation 13:1–5. Satanically empowered, it will be ruled finally by the Antichrist. The whole world will follow him and worship him. The saints will refuse, resulting in the martyrdom of millions of them, but in the end, it is they who will inherit the earth (Dan 7:7, 17–18, 23).

The renegade kingdoms established by man oppose God and his plans, but God has allowed their establishment and will eventually establish his own kingdom, replacing their rule. The final form of this "Roman" empire will have a European base, as Rome did, and will include the Arab nations of northern Africa and the Middle East. Eventually it will involve the whole world, a form of political globalization, or a transnational state apparatus. The beast will have ten horns, perhaps representing the leaders of the most powerful countries, comparable to the G20 countries today. The Antichrist will uproot three of them when he comes to power.

There is a lot of economic, social and political integration happening in the world today; the possibility of a single world empire is great, if not inevitable. It will be driven by ever-developing technology, faster transport and communications, and multiculturalism – more than half the population growth in western countries is currently due to migration. The European Union currently has twenty-eight states and there are ongoing negotiations with a dozen more.

Babylon is a symbolic name representing world dominion. It will include all the megacities of the world which will be interconnected and united together by banks, share markets, shipping, airlines, trade pacts, political alliances and the internet. The world system is characterized by pride, greed, corruption, immorality and godlessness. In a single day, at the end of the age, the cities will collapse, and Babylon will fall. This is the Fall of Babylon, described in Revelation 17–18.

7. THE RESURRECTION OF THE RIGHTEOUS

Jesus said all who are in the graves will hear his voice and come out, those who have done good will rise to life, those who have done evil will rise to condemnation (John 5:28–29). Believers will be resurrected before the millennium and unbelievers will come to life after the millennium (Rev 20:5). There is ample evidence to support two resurrections. The first resurrection involves the *righteous* (Luke 14:14), *those who are considered worthy* of taking part in it (Luke 20:35–36), *those who belong to Christ* (1 Cor 15:23), and *those who don't worship the beast* (Rev 20:5).

Those who are resurrected before the millennium receive rewards for what they have done. Their sins are forgiven, so they are not judged or condemned in any way. The wicked dead will be raised at the end of the world and judged according to what they have done. The sea will give up its dead and Death and Hades will give up their dead, and all those whose names are not written in the Lamb's book of life will be consigned to hell. There is no evidence that the wicked are resurrected in bodily form. The resurrection body is a glorified supernatural body, which is not appropriate for the wicked. So, their punishment in hell should not be regarded as physical pain; it is more likely to be the mental anguish and remorse of having sinned against God in whom they refused to believe, and on missing out on his blessings; the resurrection, the New Jerusalem, the renewed creation and eternal life. Satan and his demons will also be damned and excluded from God's paradise.

Although the physical creation will be restored to its original condition, it is only redeemed humanity who will enjoy a glorious resurrection. The creation will be liberated from its bondage to decay and brought into the glorious freedom of the children of God (Rom 8:21). Irrational creatures will not be glorified as redeemed humanity will be. For them, it is the survival and health of the species that is important, not the resurrection of the individual. The righteous will be resurrected at the last day (John 6:39), that is, the last day of this age, when the Messiah returns (Matt 24:30–31, 1 Thess 4:14–17, Rev 1:7, 14.14–16) on the clouds of heaven with power and great glory.

All mankind dies because of the sin of Adam. All mankind will be resurrected because of Christ's victory. He is the one who raises the dead (John 11:25). Resurrections occur on three different occasions. Jesus was the first person to be resurrected after the crucifixion, then at his coming those who have died 'in Christ' (1 Cor 15:23), and finally, the resurrection of the wicked after the millennium (Rev 20:5).

What actually happens when Jesus returns and the dead are resurrected? The souls of Christians who have died are with Jesus in heaven. Their bodies have decayed in their graves, but their souls are no longer there. Resurrection literally means 'rising', with the implication that the dead body will come to life and rise out of the grave. The body can't rise without its soul; it will return to the body at this time in the same way that it departed the body at death. Angels, spirits and resurrected people have the ability to move from one place to another instantaneously. Jesus will send his angels with a loud trumpet call, and they will gather his elect from one end of heaven to another. They will gather and guide hundreds of millions of resurrected and raptured saints back to meet the Lord in the air. Paul said that since we believe that Jesus died and rose again, even so, through Jesus, God will *bring with him* those who have fallen asleep (1 Thess 4:14). The word "bring" shows us that Jesus will continue to descend to earth. He is not taking the resurrected back to heaven. Bodies are meant for life on earth.

The resurrection will happen everywhere on earth where there are dead bodies or remains of believers. Christ, by the power that enables him to bring everything under his control, will transform whatever is left of these lowly bodies so that they will be like his glorious body (Phil 3:21). Natural bodies are buried, but they are raised as spiritual, supernatural bodies (1 Cor 15:44). It is important to believe that our bodies will be resurrected; our future existence is not as bodiless souls.

We are to eagerly await our adoption as sons, the redemption of our bodies (Rom 8:23). We became children of God at conversion when we were redeemed by the blood of Christ, but we will not be completely transformed until the body is redeemed. To be genuine sons of God, we need to have supernatural immortal bodies like that which Christ now possesses.

After a believer dies, he is away from the body and home with the Lord (2 Cor 5:8). Now at the resurrection, the Lord will bring the resurrected and raptured saints with him back to the earth. Clothed with their resurrection bodies, they will reign on earth (Rev 5:10). Jesus said we should not be afraid of those who kill the body but cannot kill the soul. From the foundation of the world, God has prepared a kingdom (*monarchy*) for us to inherit and possess (Matt 25:34).

It is God who raises the dead, but each member of the Trinity has a role. Jesus is the resurrection and the life. It is he who raises the dead bodies of believers (John 11:25–26). As he is the Creator (John 1:3–4, 1 Cor 8:6, Col 1:16, Heb 1:2), resurrecting the body is no problem for him. It will happen instantaneously, in the wink of an eye; the dead saints will be raised, and the living saints will be changed (1 Cor 15:51–52). Paul spoke of the Spirit's role in the resurrection of the living, when he said that if the Spirit of him who raised Jesus from the dead lives in us, he will also give life to our mortal bodies, through his Spirit who lives in us (Rom 8:11).

8. The Resurrection Body

The resurrection body is supernatural. It is a spiritual body: immortal, imperishable, glorious and powerful. And heavenly, because the resurrected will bear the image of the man from heaven. The Lord will return to be glorified in his saints, and to be marveled at by them (2 Thess 1:10). Jesus said that he is glorified in them (John 17:10). They will enhance his glory, when they are glorified by their resurrection and their redeemed state in the New Jerusalem.

There are two bodies, the natural and the spiritual. The natural body is suited to the physical creation; planet earth. The spiritual body is suited to another sphere or dimension, what we usually call heaven, but, more specifically, our future destination is the New Jerusalem which will come down from God out of heaven. We will have the ability to live in the New Jerusalem in a spiritual dimension in our supernatural, spiritual bodies, and also to appear on earth in natural bodies in our role as rulers and priests for God in the Messiah's kingdom.

Resurrection bodies are supernatural, capable of existing in heaven and earth, just as Jesus did during the forty days after his resurrection. His body was material while on earth; his disciples touched him and he ate fish in their presence (Luke 24:39–43). They are also supernatural, spiritual, immortal bodies.

Paul likens the dead body to a seed that is sown and the resurrected body to the plant that grows from it. There will be continuity from seed to plant. The continuity may be carried by our DNA, the carrier of genetic information: the fundamental and distinctive characteristics or qualities of a person. But, just as an oak tree is far more glorious than the acorn from which it sprouted, so our resurrection bodies will be more glorious than our present bodies. We will bear the image of the man from heaven (1Cor 15:48–49). Unless a person is born again, he will not see or enter the kingdom of God (John 3:3, 5), and unless he is resurrected, he cannot inherit the kingdom of God (1 Cor 15:50), ample evidence that we are not yet in the kingdom. Both amillennialists and premillennialists will fail to interpret this verse correctly, until they accept the truth that entering the kingdom means entering a kingship, becoming part of the Messiah's monarchy. Subjects of the messianic kingdom will be flesh and blood people, because they will live in the physical creation, but those who constitute the monarchy will have supernatural bodies, because they will live in the New Jerusalem.

Absent from the body, at home with the Lord (2 Cor 5:8) implies that Christians go to heaven when they die. How should we envisage heaven? In the parable of the rich man and Lazarus, when Lazarus dies, Jesus said he was carried by the angels to Abraham's side. This is a reunion with other believers already in heaven. In Hebrews 12:22–24, believers are told that they have come to Mount Zion, to the heavenly Jerusalem, the city of the living God. Then, in Revelation 14:1, John saw a vision of the Lamb standing on Mount Zion with the symbolic 144,000 people of God. They are singing before God's throne.

The Lord is seen as descending from heaven on a white horse, and the armies of heaven are with him (Rev 19:11). These are the resurrected saints, arrayed in fine linen, already defined as the righteous deeds of the saints. The resurrected saints will reign with Christ for a thousand years; the second death has no power over them. They are priests of God and of Christ. Jesus will strike down the nations and rule them with a rod of iron (Rev 19:15), and he'll give the saints who are with him authority over the nations, so they also will rule them with a rod of iron. There is no mention of going back to heaven; the destiny of the righteous is to reign over the earth. Our future habitation is the New Jerusalem, the city of the living God. The glorified saints will live together with God, the judge of all, Jesus, the mediator of a new covenant, and innumerable angels.

9. The Rapture of the Living Saints

The Lord *himself* will descend bodily from heaven with a cry of command, and the redeemed dead will hear his voice and rise from the dead. Then Christians who are still alive on earth will be caught up together with them in the clouds to meet the Lord in the air. From that moment on, clothed in their resurrection bodies, they will be with the Lord forever. The unbelieving dead will also hear the voice of the Son of God one day, but this clearly occurs after the millennium (Rev 20:5).

The passage which gives most detail about the rapture is 1 Thessalonians 4:13–17. The New Testament nowhere teaches that Jesus will return on two occasions, one secret and one public. The context of the Lord's return is a visible, noisy, public occasion, accompanied by the resurrection of the dead saints and the rapture of the living saints. It follows immediately after the distress and the cosmic signs at the end of the Great Tribulation (Matt 24:30–31).

Jesus will continue his descent to earth and then go and defeat the Antichrist (Rev 19:11–14) and save Israel and redeem. The armies of heaven, arrayed in fine linen, are the saints who accompany Jesus as he descends to earth to defeat the armies at Armageddon. These saints may number a billion or more.

As for those who are raptured, two men will be in the field, one will be taken and one left. Two women will be grinding at the mill, one will be taken and one left (Matt 24:41). There will be two in one bed, one will be taken and the other left (Luke 17:34). They will rise and meet the Lord in the air. Whoever tries to keep his life (by worshiping the Antichrist) will lose it and whoever loses his life (in martyrdom) will preserve it (Luke 17:33).

Where to from the air? Forever with the Lord. Why is Jesus returning? To reign over the earth as the promised Messiah. The last book of the Bible is the revelation of Jesus Christ which God gave him to show his servants what must soon take place (Rev 1:1). It is an unveiling at the same time of what must soon take place and of the Messiah himself. If the Messiah returns to earth solely to resurrect the saints and whisk them off to heaven, he is not being revealed. If he returns to earth to reign over it for a thousand years and to restore it, he will be revealed to the whole of mankind, to all of creation and to the spiritual world, both good and evil.

10. The Marriage Feast of the Lamb

After the saints are resurrected, the marriage feast of the Lamb is celebrated. It is a symbolic wedding ceremony, celebrating the union of Christ and his community (Rev 19:6–9). This union is portrayed symbolically by the New Jerusalem (Rev 21:2 – 22:5), prepared as a bride adorned for her husband. This is a picture of Christ and his church. The saints will live forever after in union with their Lord, whether reigning on earth during the millennium, or reigning throughout eternity.

John said that the saints will reign with Christ for a thousand years (Rev 20:4), but where will they live? The New Jerusalem is a city prepared for the bride and her husband. This is their dwelling place and God himself will be with them and be their God (Rev 21:2–4). The holy city comes down out of heaven from God, so the saints will not live in heaven. The destination of the city is not specified, but as the saints will be resurrected people with supernatural bodies, the holy city which descends from heaven will not be a part of this earth. Rather, it will be above the earth, in close correspondence with the earthly Jerusalem (Isa 60:1–2, 19–20, 62:1–2). Or it may be envisaged as being identical with the earthly Jerusalem, but in a different sphere or dimension.

The resurrected people won't marry or be in a human marriage relationship (Luke 20:34–36); they will be married to the Lord. But there will be continuity between the natural and the supernatural. People will be recognizable. After the resurrection, Jesus appeared to his disciples during a 40–day period and this gives us a basis to think about our own mode of existence during the millennium. He had a body that his disciples recognized, but at times people doubted (Matt 28, Mark 16, Luke 24, John 20–21). He talked to them, ate with them, and they were invited to touch him. He suddenly appeared to them in a locked room, and he prepared a meal for them by the lake, producing fire and bread and fish from nowhere. On the other hand, in several appearances, his disciples didn't immediately recognize him. His recognition seemed to be under his own control. We can conclude that he had a physical, recognizable body with supernatural powers of appearing and disappearing to another dimension. And we will be like him.

The vision of the New Jerusalem with all the jewels and huge cubic dimensions is symbolic. The details should not be taken literally, but every detail has a meaning. The vision expresses the great size of the city and its great glory. The city is called the bride, because the city is equivalent to its inhabitants – it is the community of the redeemed; those whose names are written in the Lamb's book of life. The city has a great size because her inhabitants number in the hundreds of millions. It is glorious with the glory of God himself, who dwells there with redeemed humanity. He is their God and they are his people. He is their Father and they are his children. They are the bride of Christ and he is the husband. It is one big family, a royal family, and they reign together.

If the holy city, the New Jerusalem, is the bride of Christ, when did it begin? F. F. Bruce says the city has existed eternally in heaven (The Epistle to the Hebrews p. 374). It is surely better to think of God as dwelling in a city than sitting on a cloud. Believers have already come to the city of the living God. They haven't seen it, but they have come to a spiritual realm, to innumerable angels joyfully gathered together, to the community of the firstborn whose names are enrolled in heaven, to God, the judge of all, to the spirits of the righteous made perfect, to Jesus, the mediator of a new covenant, and to his sprinkled blood (Heb 12:22–24). We have come to it, but in our mortal bodies, we cannot enter yet. As the spirits of the righteous are there, it seems probable that this holy city in the spiritual realm is our destination when we die, the so-called intermediate state. Abraham, Isaac and Jacob are there.

John saw the Holy City prepared as a bride beautifully dressed for her husband (Rev 21:2, 9–11). The elect are called the bride of the Lamb (Rev 19:7, 21:9), but in Revelation 21:3 the emphasis is on God himself, who is going to live with them. They will be his people and he will be their God. The throne of God will no longer be in heaven; it will be in the holy city. This is our final state when we will be united to God.

Can, maybe a billion people, live in a cube as described? How can we serve our God and rule the world, if we are all concentrated in the one city? The description of the New Jerusalem is symbolic, the details are not revealed. But we will reign with the Messiah on his throne (Rev 3:21) and we will reign over the earth (Ap 5:10) for one thousand years (Ap 20:4).

The wedding ceremony, formally uniting the Messiah and his bride will take place in the air, when the city comes down out of heaven from God. The descent of the New Jerusalem will constitute the inauguration of the messianic kingdom (Isa 11:10b, 62:1–5, 12, Zech 14:5c, 8–9). There the Messiah will have his throne (Rev 22:3), and there the church will rest, and feast, and reign with her Lord.

The elders and living creatures worship God and cry "Hallelujah" because the Lord their God reigns (Rev 19). Then they declare that the marriage of the Lamb has come, and his bride has made herself ready. The happy bride dressed in fine white linen is none other than the church or the saints; those who accepted the gospel invitation.

Paul alluded to this marriage when he exhorted husbands to love their wives as the Messiah loved the church and gave himself for it (Eph 5:25–27). He spoke of marriage as a union: a man leaves his father and mother and is united with his wife, and the two become one flesh. It's a great mystery, because marriage symbolizes the union between the Messiah and the church (Eph 5:31–32). The New Jerusalem is not depicted as a city of buildings; it's a community of people united to God. This community is represented by the names of the twelve tribes of Israel and the names of the twelve apostles, indicating that it consists of believers from Israel and all the nations, but the Israel of the millennium won't be gloried until the end of the millennium and the last judgment.

11. JESUS' DESCENT TO EARTH

The Messiah will arrive in great glory (Rev 19:11–16) with his angels and the saints who will be resurrected (Rev 14:14–16) and the living saints who will be raptured. He will empower the remnant of Israel and they will defeat the world's armies gathered at Jerusalem. The birds are called to feed on the carcasses (Rev 19:17–18) after this great slaughter. It is at this time that Israel will be saved (Rev 1:7, Zech 12:6, 10).

Jesus will descend to the Mount of Olives on the eastern side of Jerusalem. The Mount of Olives will split in two from east to west, forming a very large valley, with half of the mountain moving toward the north and half toward the south (Zech 14:4). The apostles were on the Mount of Olives at the ascension when the angels told them that Jesus would return in the same way they saw him go up into heaven (Acts 1:11–12). The Mount of Olives is east of Jerusalem just across the Kidron valley.

From the Mount of Olives, the Messiah will enter Jerusalem and the temple via the east gate (Ezek 43:1–5). Ezekiel saw the Lord's coming in a vision. He said his coming sounded like the roar of rushing water and the earth was radiant with his glory. It will be very noisy and be accompanied by brilliant light. When the glory of the Lord entered the temple in Jerusalem, the Lord told Ezekiel that this was the place of his throne and the place for the soles of his feet. He would live there among Israel forever (Ezek 43:7). Ezekiel's vision of the glory of the God of Israel is nothing else but the return of the Messiah. The place for the soles of his feet is his point of contact with the earth there in the temple where he will be worshiped.

The "prince" spoken about by Ezekiel is often seen to be the Messiah, but if so, he is spoken about in very muted terms. As he is spoken about as having sons, I interpret him as being ruler of Israel during the millennium. Israel, like all the nations on earth will have their own rulers.

12. The New Jerusalem

The New Jerusalem is the city of the redeemed, and they will take up residence there as soon as they are resurrected. The holy city symbolizes the community of the saints and their union with Christ and God. John saw the holy city coming down out of heaven (Rev 21:2). It doesn't need the light of the sun or the moon; it is not part of the physical creation. Its light comes from the glory of God and the Lamb whose throne is in it. John tells us that the nations will walk by its light and the kings of the earth will bring their splendor to it (Rev 21:24). There is a correspondence between the earthly Jerusalem and the New Jerusalem, so these statements should be interpreted in accordance with Isaiah's prophecies. Isaiah said that in the last days, the mountain of the Lord's temple would be established as the highest of mountains. It will be raised above the hills and all nations will stream to it. Many groups will go to the temple of the God of Jacob, so that they might learn his ways and walk in his paths (Isa 2:2–3). And to earthly Jerusalem Isaiah said: "Arise, shine, for your light has come, and the glory of *the Lord rises upon you*. See, darkness covers the earth and thick darkness is over the peoples, but the Lord rises upon you, and *his glory appears over you*. Nations will come to your light, and kings to the brightness of your dawn" (Isa 60:1–3 NIV). He is saying that the Lord's glory will be visible over Jerusalem and the nations will come to the light and kings will bring their gifts to it (Rev 21:24–27).

The Lord's glory and throne are in the New Jerusalem which will, in some intimate way, be connected with the earthly Jerusalem, which will be surrounded by its light. The coming of the Lord will produce a significant celestial change over Jerusalem, which will remain for the duration of the millennium. Isaiah prophesied a new sky as well as a new earth. Zechariah said, when the Lord comes, the daylight will be neither bright nor overcast. It will be a unique day, known only to the Lord, neither daytime nor nighttime, and at evening time there will be light! (Zech 14:6–7).

The poor man who was carried to Abraham's bosom will be in the New Jerusalem. This city is the home of the redeemed, but it is not in the physical dimension; it is not a part of this creation. There is no sun and moon there, no night, nothing accursed or unclean. The throne of God and the Lamb is there. God exists everywhere, but this will be his home, together with his redeemed. They will see his face. God told Moses that man could not see him and live, but later, Jesus said that the pure in heart would see God (Mat 5:8). In this spiritual dimension, we will be like God and we will see him.

This city is the New Jerusalem which comes down out of heaven from God prepared as a bride for her husband (Rev 21:2). The catalyst for the descent is that the spirits of the righteous are to be embodied. They will no longer be incorporeal spirits, they will be reunited with immortal, supernatural bodies. In Matthew 24:30–31, the resurrection is pictured as the Messiah returning with power and great glory, sending out his angels to the ends of the earth to gather the elect. In reality the spirits of the dead are in the holy city, not in their graves. After they are embodied, they will meet the Lord in the air. It will happen in the blink of an eye. Then the living will be gathered up and transformed (raptured). All will descend with the Messiah to Jerusalem together with the angels. This is the second coming. The Lord descends from heaven with a cry of command, with the voice of an archangel and with the sound of the trumpet of God, then the dead in Christ will rise first, then those who are alive will meet the Lord in the air and they will always be with the Lord (1 Thess 4:17).

John was carried away in the Spirit to a great, high mountain and he saw the holy city coming down out of heaven from God, *having the glory of God* (Rev 21:10–11a). In a vision, Ezekiel saw *the glory of the God of Israel* coming from the east, and the sound of his coming was like the sound of many waters, and the earth shone with *his glory* (Ezek 43:2). Is this not the same event, the return of Jesus Christ?

The holy city is the New Jerusalem, different from the earthly Jerusalem, the capital of the nation of Israel. Only the resurrected whose names are written in the Lamb's book of life can enter the New Jerusalem. Earthly Jerusalem has a temple and its gates are open continually, so that people may bring the wealth of the nations into it (Isa 60:11).

Revelation 21–22 is often interpreted as following the Last Judgment. But the visions John saw are not always chronological. The descriptions of judgments on the world as portrayed by the seals, the trumpets and the bowls of wrath all terminate with the coming of the Messiah. Chapter 12 takes us back to the birth of Christ. The description of the New Jerusalem (Rev 21:2–22:5) is appropriately left until last because it is a description of the eternal state. There is only one verse which speaks of the new sky and earth (Rev 21:1). It is a mistake to interpret this as the creation of a new planet to replace planet earth which has disappeared (Rev 20:11). The Bible has nothing to say about a new creation. The original prophecy of a new sky and earth (Isa 65:17–25) referred to a regenerated or recreated earth, not a new creation. The new earth that God will make will endure for a long time and all humanity will go to Jerusalem to worship him (Isa 66:22–24). It is the millennium.

How will all humanity go and worship the Lord? Will the Messiah be physically present on earth, or does all humanity come to worship at his temple at Jerusalem where he is present spiritually? The Jewish expectation was always to have a physically present Messiah, and Jesus told his disciples that at the renewal of all things, he would sit on his glorious throne, so, they would expect to see him here on earth. Zechariah says that his feet will stand on the Mount of Olives, which means a physical appearance at his coming. Ezekiel saw the glory of the God of Israel coming from the east and entering the temple in Jerusalem (Ezek 43:1–5), and Zechariah said that the Lord would be King over the whole earth, and that the unredeemed survivors from all the nations would come to worship him year after year at Jerusalem (Zech 14:9, 16).

When the saints are resurrected, they will meet the Lord in the air, and they will be forever with the Lord as he begins the millennial reign. The souls of dead believers have been with the Lord in the heavenly Jerusalem since they died, but now all God's people will meet him in the air in their resurrection bodies. Where to from here? Paul said that when the Lord Jesus is revealed from heaven in blazing fire with his mighty angels, he will come to be glorified by (or in) his saints and to be marveled at by all who believe (2 Thess 1:7, 10). John saw the holy city coming down out of heaven, prepared as a bride beautifully dressed for her husband (Rev 21:2). The community of the saved have come down to earth with the Messiah and have received their resurrection bodies on the way. They have been joined by the living saints who were gathered up by the angels. This is the descent of the New Jerusalem from heaven to earth that John saw. The city consists of its inhabitants: the redeemed, the angels and God himself. Now the dwelling of God is with humans. He will make his home with them and they will be his people (Rev 21:3). The dimensions of the city are given as twelve-thousand stadia cube. That is about 1,380 miles cube. The city is in another dimension, so these dimensions are simply symbolic of its immense size or capacity. It doesn't need the light of the sun or the moon. The glory of the Lord, whose throne is in the city, will give it light and this light will be visible over the earthly Jerusalem (Isa 4:5, 52:7–10, 60:2–3).

Abraham was looking forward to this city that has foundations, whose designer and builder is God (Heb 11:10). No record or tradition of this hope is given in the Old Testament, but we know that he was a man of incredible faith. He had the promise of the land and the promise that all the families of the earth would be blessed "in him". These promises will be fulfilled in the millennium. Israel will be extended to the full borders as promised, and the saints from all nations will be glorified and will rule the world in union with the Messiah, Jesus, Abraham's descendant (Matt 1:1).

The Holy City is a symbolic representation of our glorified eternal state which begins at the resurrection. It will be our home during the millennium and on into eternity. The descent of the New Jerusalem that John saw (Rev 21:10–11, 24) suggests that this other worldly city will be visible as a bright light above the earthly Jerusalem. Although the description of the city is symbolic in nature, its descent is an historical event. Isaiah said that the Lord would create over the entire site of Mount Zion, including those who assemble there, a cloud by day, and smoke and the glow of a flaming fire by night (Isa 4:5). This description is to be taken literally. When the Israelites wandered in the wilderness, the Lord went in front of them by day in a pillar of cloud to lead them along the way, and by night in a pillar of fire to give them light (Exod 13:21). When he came down on Sinai, the mountain was completely enveloped in smoke, because he had come down in fire on it (Exod 19:18). These manifestations of the Lord's glory occurred physically, and another one is prophesied to occur over the millennial Jerusalem.

The light shining from the New Jerusalem when the Messiah reigns on Mount Zion and in Jerusalem will cause the moon to be confounded and the sun to be ashamed. In other words, his glory will be brighter than that of sun or moon (Isa 24:23). The nations will be drawn to the light of Jerusalem, and their unbelieving kings will come and serve Jerusalem's inhabitants. They will bring their wealth, and if they don't serve them, they will perish. Israel's traditional oppressors will now submit to them. The Messiah and his saints will rule them with a rod of iron, and they will be forced to acknowledge that Jerusalem is the city of Israel's God (Isa 60:3, 14).

The New Jerusalem is first mentioned in Revelation 3:12, where Jesus declares that he will make the overcomers pillars in God's temple. He will write God's name on them, and the name of the New Jerusalem, and his own new name. The focus is on belonging to God and Jesus and being a member of the messianic community.

Our union with Christ results in a celestial redeemed community called the New Jerusalem. It is a supernatural state with some continuity with the garden of Eden. Jesus told the thief who expressed faith in him on the cross that he would be with him in *paradise* that very day. He also told the overcomers in the church at Ephesus that he would give them the right to eat from *the tree of life which is in the paradise of God*. The Jews believed that the garden of Eden was paradise, and that it was always present somewhere. The paradise of Revelation is New Jerusalem. The tree of life which bears fruit every month is there, and its leaves are for the healing of the nations. The river of the water of life symbolizes eternal life with all its blessings. So, our future abode can be thought of as a glorious city or a restful riverside park; they are both symbolic representations of eternal life.

13. Armageddon

When the sixth bowl is poured out on the Euphrates river, it opens the way for the kings of the east and the kings of the whole world to gather in Israel for the battle of Armageddon. This gathering of armies may take months. Their destruction by the Lord is described (Rev 14:17–20, 19:19–22).

Armageddon is a symbolic name for a great battlefield. It represents a gathering of the armies of the nations who will go and fight against Jerusalem (Rev 16:16). Satanically inspired, they will be anti-Christian, anti-Israeli, anti-God forces gathering for the battle on the great day of God (Ps 2:2–3, Rev 16:14). The kings of the earth take their stand and the rulers conspire together against the Lord and his Messiah, while the One enthroned in heaven laughs and scoffs at them, and then terrifies them in his anger. Great numbers from the east and north will come to fight in Israel, but godless mankind will be slaughtered. These armies will end up attacking one another in a great battle that is centered in the Middle East (Zech 12:1–9, 14:12–15). At the same time the world's megacities will be destroyed by nuclear warfare and a massive earthquake.

Joel said that there has never been anything like this army before, and there will never be one like them again (Joel 2:2–5.). Before the army comes, the land is like the garden of Eden; after they leave, there is only a barren wasteland. It will a great army of cavalry and tanks and weapons of modern warfare.

At this time, there will be signs in the heavens, and on the earth blood, fire, and columns of smoke. The sun will become dark, and the moon red, before the coming of the great and terrifying Day of the Lord. This is Armageddon. Joel continues his description of the judgment of the nations, which terminates in the coming of the Lord, bringing victory for his people. There will be multitudes in the valley of judgment, and then the Lord will roar from Zion, and shout from Jerusalem and give victory to Israel.

The Lord is calling all the nations to gather their armies and come to Israel for a time of judgment. But why are all the nations going there? Ezekiel 38–39 describe an invasion of a resettled Israel in the last days by an international leader called Gog of the land of Magog. The Israelis who have returned from many nations have transformed their promised land and are living there securely. But there will be an invasion from the north, possibly a coalition of Muslim countries supported by Russia. The recent civil war in Syria has brought many of Israel's enemies closer to their northern border.

These nations will surround Jerusalem in an effort to exterminate the Jewish nation from the earth. Zechariah 14:2 tells us that Jerusalem will be captured by these forces, the houses ransacked, and the women raped. God will allow Jerusalem to be entered and two thirds of the people to be defeated, but at the climax of the battle, the Messiah will return to completely annihilate the invading armies.

Half the city will go into exile, but the rest of the people will not be taken from the city. It is while this battle is taking place that Jesus will return and defeat them.

The Lord will be Israel's strength at this battle of Armageddon, but how does he give them the victory? Zechariah tells us that the Lord will inflict the opposing forces with panic and madness. They will attack each other and the Jewish forces will devour them (Zech 12:4–9, 14:13–15). The Lord will inflict them with a plague; their flesh will rot away, their eyes will rot in their sockets, and their tongues to rot in their mouths.

At the same time there will be a massive *earthquake* throughout the land of Israel, the greatest earthquake that has ever occurred. Every living creature and all the peoples on the face of the earth will quake at the Lord's presence. Mountains will collapse and every wall will fall to the ground. Every weapon of war will be turned against fellow soldiers. God will shower the vast armies with hailstones, fire and sulfur. Everyone will come to know that the returning Messiah is Almighty God (Ezek 38:18–23).

The effects of this *earthquake* are graphically recorded after the sixth seal is broken: The sun will turn black, the moon will turn dark red, stars (missiles, meteorites?) will fall to the earth. The sky will vanish as if being rolled up, and every mountain and island will move from its place. The world leaders and important people, the generals, the rich and powerful, the slave and free will conceal themselves in caves and among the rocks in the mountains trying to escape from God and his Messiah. It is the great day of their wrath and nobody can endure it, except the redeemed. Then the seventh angel will throw the contents of his bowl across the sky, and the great city "Babylon" that has dominion over the kings of the earth will split into three parts, and all *the cities of the nations will collapse.* Islands will vanish, and mountains will no longer be recognizable. Huge hailstones will fall on people whose only response will be to curse God (Rev 16:12–21).

This great judgment on the day of the Lord is also described by the prophet Isaiah, who emphasizes that the entire inhabited earth will be turned into a desolation with the purpose of annihilating the sinners in it. God will make people scarcer than pure gold (Isa 13:6–13).

Jesus confirmed the interpretation of these prophecies and added that all the tribes of the land will mourn when they see the Son of Man coming on the clouds of heaven with power and great glory (Matt 24:29–30). He seems to have in mind the prophecy made by Zechariah about Israel's conversion (Zech 12:10–14). It is not the nations of the world who are beating their breasts in repentance at the Messiah's coming! The Greek word for "earth" and "land" is the same. In Zechariah 12:12 it is very clearly the clans of Israel who are mourning, not the nations of the world, who can only curse God.

Zechariah emphasizes the siege made against Jerusalem and Judah by all the nations of the earth. He said the Lord will make Jerusalem an unstable cup for all the surrounding armies. It will be a heavy weight; everyone who burdens themselves with it will be crushed. The Lord will strike every horse with panic and every rider with insanity. He will protect Judah and destroy all the nations who come against Jerusalem (Zech 12:1–4, 9). He adds that Jerusalem will be captured, the houses ransacked, the women raped, and half of the city will go into exile. Then the Lord will destroy all of the nations that attack Jerusalem. He will cause their flesh to rot away, even while they're standing on their feet, their eyes to rot in their sockets, and their tongues to rot in their mouths. The armies will panic and attack each other (Zech 14:2, 12–15).

That is Armageddon! Let us, the redeemed, be thankful that we are receiving a kingdom that cannot be shaken.

14. Israel's Conversion

The final seven years of this age will give Israel and Jerusalem great prominence. Israel is already counted among the top ten most powerful nations of the world.

The future conversion of the nation of Israel as a whole is clearly prophesied in many scriptures. The question in focus here is when will this conversion take place and who will it involve. The relevant verses will be given. During the millennium, the Messiah will be king, and the resurrected church will be reigning with him over the survivors of the Great Tribulation from all over the world. Israel, on the other hand, will continue as a nation on earth, ruled over by their Messiah.

In Paul's three-chapter discussion of Israel in Romans 9–11, he states that stubbornness will be upon Israel until the full number of converts from other nations comes to faith. Then, all Israel will be saved, just as the prophets said they would. The Deliverer will come from Zion and remove ungodliness from Jacob (Rom 11:25–27). Romans 11:12 speaks of the benefit "their fullness" will bring. When all Israel is saved, meaning the full number of Israelites alive at that time, the Messiah will rule from Jerusalem over his redeemed nation Israel, and from there his reign will extend to the four corners of the earth.

Ezekiel said the Lord would restore the fortunes of Jacob and show mercy to the *entire* house of Israel. He will not leave any of them remaining among the nations when he pours out his Spirit on Israel (Ezek 39:25, 28–29). Ezekiel makes it clear that this salvation is post Armageddon, a spiritual conversion, and it involves the land of Israel into which they will be regathered. The Messiah will be king over them, and they will live according to God's rules. They, with their children and grandchildren, will live forever in the land that God gave Jacob, the land where their ancestors lived. The Lord will establish them, increase their population and place his temple among them, so that the nations will understand that he has set Israel apart from them (Ezek 37:24–28). This is in harmony with the premillennialist view that the Messiah will reign over the earth. His throne will be in the New Jerusalem (Rev 22:1–3) which will be seen above the old Jerusalem (Isa 60:1–3).

Over centuries past there have been opposing views of the Jewish messianic expectation. Older commentators lived in an era that preceded the return of the Jews from all over the world to form the new state of Israel in 1948, and to take control of Jerusalem again in 1967 after two thousand years of oppression. Before the return, it was difficult for many older commentators to believe it could happen, and so they interpreted the scriptures as having been fulfilled in the church. In addition, there has been historically a considerable anti-Jewish sentiment that badly biased some commentaries. Now, with the Jews restored to their land, and with the increasing prominence of Jerusalem on the world stage, the promises that they would be converted in the last days, and that Jerusalem would become the center of the world under their Messiah, is not so unbelievable. Some teach that the rule of Christ in the hearts of believers has replaced the old idea of a messianic kingdom on earth, but that teaching has no scriptural basis. No verse of scripture says or implies that the kingdom of God is simply the rule of Christ in our hearts.

The prophecies concerning the coming of the Messiah, a glorified Jerusalem, and the conversion of Israel are amply confirmed in both the Old and New Testaments. Israel will one day turn to the Lord *en masse,* but not before Jesus returns and the resurrection of the church takes place. They will enter the millennium as mortal survivors of the Great Tribulation, not as part of the resurrected church. In their rejection of Jesus at his first coming, they forfeited their right to the kingdom, so when the Messiah rules the world with his resurrected saints, only a tiny percentage of them will be Jewish. Israel will be God's special people on earth during the millennium. God's call is irrevocable. They will be converted after Jesus' return, and all those living among the nations will return to Israel. God will be vindicated as the God of Israel, and the Father of Jesus the Messiah, who will rule as King of kings and Lord of lords.

There will be a new temple in the earthly Jerusalem where Israel will worship, and the nations of the world will come to acknowledge the Lord and to bring their resources as an offering. Earthly Jerusalem will be glorified. It will be raised up physically and the light of the glory of God will shine forth from the New Jerusalem which will be above it. Let those who say that the prophets of the Old Testament knew nothing of a millennium re-evaluate what Isaiah said when he spoke about the creation of a new sky and earth (Isa 65:17–25). Isaiah was talking about a renewal of the present earth during the millennium. Cf. Isa 66:22–23, Joel 3:17–18, Zech 14:9–11. Jesus called it the renewal of all things (Matt 19:28).

Israel will be saved in the same way as the Gentiles are, through faith in Jesus the Messiah. They will become part of the body of Christ, the bride of Christ, but as their conversion occurs after Jesus' return, they will not be resurrected until the end of the millennium.

When the Deliverer comes from Zion and banishes ungodliness from Jacob, then all Israel will be saved (Rom 11:26). It is not only the Jews living in Israel who are saved, but every Jew on the planet. In 2018 there were an estimated 14.5 million Jews in the world, 6.45 million of whom were living in Israel and 5.7 million in the US.

After the Messiah returns to Zion and defeats the surrounding armies, he will pour out his Spirit on all the surviving inhabitants of Jerusalem and Israel, and he will gather the Jews who remain from among the nations (Isa 60:4, 9). Many other verses speak of the return of the exiles at this time (Isa 11:10–12, 27:12–13, 49:22, 56:8, 66:19–20). The Lord will reach out his hand a second time to reclaim the remnant that is left of his people (Isa 11:11).

As all these returning Jews will be unbelievers at the time of Messiah's arrival, they will not be resurrected and be part of the monarchy in Messiah's kingdom. They will be Jewish subjects in the Messiah's kingdom and will have the great privilege of being the Messiah's own people. They will serve as priests and Levites at the temple in Jerusalem.

Zechariah prophesied about the Jews who will return and live in Jerusalem. He said, there will be old men and old women sitting in the parks of Jerusalem, each one of them holding canes due to their old age. The city parks will be filled with boys and girls. They will play in the city's open parks (Zech 8:3–5). Zechariah is not talking here about resurrected people. The resurrection body will probably have an age of 25–35 years old, when people are in their prime, not old or young, and certainly not holding canes. There will no longer be in Jerusalem a young boy who lives only a few days, or an old person who does not live out his days. One who falls short of a hundred years will be considered accursed (Isa 65:20). So, those who will dwell in Jerusalem during the millennium will be saved, but not resurrected. Zechariah said that after the Lord has saved his people from the land of the east and from the land of the west, he will bring them back to live in Jerusalem. They will be his people and he will be their God (Zech 8:7–8).

The time of Israel's conversion is important. If they were to be converted before the return of Jesus, then they would become part of the church, as many Jews have done over the centuries. We live is the age of grace, from Pentecost to the Second Coming, wherein people of every tribe and language are invited to put their faith in Jesus Christ, to be born again and united to Christ. When Jesus arrives, the door will be shut (Matt 25:11–12). While Jesus is in the air, he will send out his angels and the dead believers will be resurrected. They will rise from among the dead and meet the Lord in the air, and from that point on they will be forever with the Lord. There are no scriptures that say believers will go to heaven at this time. The Lord's activity for the following thousand years is to do with the earth. Believers who are still alive at the Lord's coming will be raptured, caught up into the clouds with the risen dead. Then the Messiah will continue his descent to planet earth as described in Zechariah 14:3–5, 9, 16.

Jesus said the same thing in Matthew 24:29–31. After the troubles of those days, the sun and moon will be darkened, the powers of heaven will be shaken loose, the sign of the Son of Man will appear in the sky, and then all the tribes of the land (Israel) will mourn when they see him coming on the clouds of heaven with power and great glory. He'll send out his angels with a loud trumpet blast, and they will gather his elect from one end of heaven to the other (Matt 24:29–31) Israel's conversion will occur after the Lord has descended to earth on the Mount of Olives. The context is the battle of Armageddon. Israel will be desperately fighting against the nations of the world who have gathered against Jerusalem. Then the Messiah will come from Zion and save Israel and destroy those armies (Rom 11:26). He will pour out on Israel a spirit of grace. *They will look to him* – the one whom they pierced (John 19:37), and *they will mourn for him*, as one mourns for an only son (Zech 12:9–10). Having seen the one their ancestors crucified coming in great power and glory to save them, they will respond with great mourning. They will be born again of the Holy Spirit. John sees Jesus coming in the clouds, and he says that every eye will see him (Rev 1:7), even (or namely) those who pierced him, and all *the tribes of the land will mourn because of him*. This is exactly what Zechariah predicted. Each family of Israel will mourn separately, wailing in repentance, because they will now realize the crime of their nation in crucifying Jesus the Messiah. The tribes who mourn refer to Israel, because that is the import of Zechariah's prophecy. In Revelation, the response of unbelievers to these last day events is only to curse God, not to mourn (Rev 16:9, 11, 21). They are certainly not beating their breasts in sorrow.

The book of Revelation is written to Christians, the seven churches of Asia, so, it does not say much about Israel during the Great Tribulation. Only the New Jerusalem is referred to specifically, not the present Jerusalem, except in Revelation 11:2, 8, where it is referred to as "the holy city" and then "the great city that is spiritually called Sodom and Egypt, where their Lord was crucified."

Israel's conversion occurs after the resurrection and rapture of the elect, too late for them to be included among the saints who are resurrected at the Lord's return. Paul said that they would not be converted until *after* the full number of Gentiles comes to faith (Rom 11:25). They will be among the survivors of the Great Tribulation and will continue to live normal lives on earth. At least half the population of the world will be destroyed during this terrible time, when an earthquake occurs that will be more powerful than any previous quake, and the cities of the nations will collapse (Rev 16:18–19). In the day of his wrath, God will make man scarcer than pure gold (Isa 13:12). Together with Israel, they will be the *subjects* of the messianic kingdom. The resurrected saints will reign with Christ as his huge royal family. All Israel will be saved, so the Messiah will be reigning over his people Israel for the first time as a redeemed and obedient nation. The nations on the other hand are unbelievers and will be ruled over with a rod of iron. They will go to Jerusalem to worship the King year by year, under threat of punishment if they do not do so. We are not told if they have the opportunity to become true believers. There will also be the possibility that the next generation of Jews will not all follow the Lord. At the last judgment, after the thousand years are over, all those who were not resurrected at the first resurrection will be resurrected and judged according to what they have done. The unbelievers will then be consigned to hell, while those whose names are written in the Lamb's book of life will join their fellow saints in the New Jerusalem.

15. The Millennium

The millennium is the thousand-year reign on earth by Jesus the Messiah, which follows immediately after his return to earth. In the Gospels, whenever Jesus spoke about the coming Kingdom of God, this millennial reign, or its king, or the saints as his royal family, was what he was talking about. The Bible says he is coming soon, and the New Testament was written over 1,900 years ago. The church is always meant to have a sense of expectancy. The Christian hope is not going to heaven; it is a keen hope that Jesus will return soon and establish his reign on earth.

Jesus is the Savior of the whole world and his followers come from every tribe, people, language and nation, but he is first and foremost the Jewish Messiah. God revealed himself to Abraham and his descendants first, and it was Abraham whom he promised would be heir of the world (Gen 17:4–8, Rom 4:13). When Jesus returns from heaven, his feet will touch down on the Mount of Olives on the eastern side of Jerusalem (Zech 14:4). Jerusalem will be the center of activities at the end of this age. The Antichrist will set himself up in the temple there and the city will be surrounded by the armies of the nations at the battle of Armageddon. When the New Jerusalem comes down from heaven, it will also descend there, because it is the same event.

A kingdom consists of a king, his monarchy, his subjects and the domain. The future king of the whole earth will be Jesus Christ the Messiah. A huge monarchy, the royal family, will consist of the elect, those chosen by God through faith in Jesus. This will be part of their glorification. The millennial government will consist of millions of people from all over the world, the community of true believers in Jesus Christ. Each one will serve in the royal priesthood according to his or her gift and God's plan. The subjects of the kingdom will be those who survive the horrific time of death and destruction during the seven years of the Great Tribulation before Jesus returns (Zech 14:16). At least half the world's population will perish at that time. When the Messiah begins his rule, Satan and his demons will no longer be there. He will be securely imprisoned, so that he can no longer deceive the nations, the surviving unbelievers.

The nation of Israel is at the center of the world, and the Messiah will rule from their capital city Jerusalem. Israel has been God's people ever since he chose Abraham and his descendants, as recorded in Genesis 12:1–3. The Messiah is Jewish and a descendant of Abraham. According to numerous Old Testament prophecies, he will reign from Jerusalem over a converted Israel. Jerusalem is the city of God, the eternal holy city chosen by God as the only place on earth for his temple. Three chapters in the book of Romans describe God's choosing of Israel as his people, their unbelief, and their subsequent salvation. Paul said that all Israel will be saved, as the prophets predicted. The Deliverer will come from Zion and *banish ungodliness* from Jacob (Rom 11:26). This is a comprehensive national conversion. Paul quotes from Isaiah 59:20 and Jeremiah 31:31–34, which focus on the conversion of ethnic Israel under a new covenant. Isaiah says the Deliver will come to Zion, but Paul's quotation says he will come from Zion, in line with Psalm 53:6. In fact Jesus will return to Zion and then he'll roar out from there to defeat Israel's enemies (Joel 3:16). Despite the vocabulary, I doubt that the Messiah will ever be visible to the subjects of the Messianic kingdom. It is the pure in heart who will see God, not the unbelievers. This time the Lord will put his law within them, he'll write it on their hearts. He'll forgive their iniquity and remember their sin no more. This will not only apply to the survivors who live in Israel and Jerusalem, but to all Jews who survive in the other nations of the world (Isa 11:11–12, 14:1–2, 43:5–7, 60:4, 9, 66:20, Zech 8:8). They will all return to the Jewish homeland.

The converted Jews will be natural inhabitants of the world during the millennium. They will be brought home to live as the people of God. They will come to Jerusalem with their wealth, assisted by the nations where they are living. They will believe in the Lord and in his Messiah. There will be old people with staff in hand in the millennial Jerusalem, and boy and girls will play in the streets. Their farms will be fruitful (Isa 65:20–25, Zech 8:3–6, 12). They won't have resurrection bodies like the Messiah's monarchy however, they will be living under a just king in truth and righteousness. During the millennium, the whole earth will be renewed and enjoy a prosperity never known before. Jerusalem and the land of Israel will be especially honored as the city and land of the king. The sky will produce its dew and the earth will produce its full yield. Jerusalem will be the center of the earth and nations will flock there to pray, to inquire of the Lord, and to worship him.

What about the New Jerusalem described in Revelation 21–22? Where does it fit in? It will be the home of the resurrected redeemed, corresponding to the earthly Jerusalem, but in a different dimension. Its glory will be seen above the earthly Jerusalem. It is the home of the resurrected saints and of the Messiah and God himself. Paul mentions the Jerusalem above in contrast to the present-day Jerusalem (Gal 4:25–26) and Abraham is said to be waiting for the city with permanent foundations, whose architect and builder is God (Heb 11:10). These men of faith in Hebrews 11 were longing for a better homeland, one that would come from heaven. In fact, it is a city that God has prepared for them (Heb 11:16). The Greek adjective "heavenly" can mean "being in heaven, belonging there, or coming from there". The third sense is relevant here. We have no permanent city here but are looking for the one that is coming (Heb 13:14). This city will come down out of heaven from God (Rev 21:2, 10). It is Mount Zion, the city of the living God, the heavenly Jerusalem (Heb 12:22). Rewards, including resurrection bodies, are always spoken of as being prepared for us in heaven, but that is not the place where we will enjoy them. As the New Jerusalem will come down *out of heaven* from God, it is poor exegesis to equate it with heaven.

There is scriptural evidence that the city, or at least its glory, will be seen above Jerusalem, shining as a bright light of the glory of God during the millennium (Isa 60:1–3). The inhabitants of the New Jerusalem will be resurrected people with immortal bodies and supernatural powers.

When Jesus was resurrected, he could walk through walls. He came and went at will for forty days, making various appearances to his disciples. He talked to them, ate with them, and they touched him. When he prepared a meal for them by the lake, where did he get the fire and the bread and the fish from? During the millennium, the saints will have bodies like Jesus' glorious resurrected body; they will move from one place to another instantaneously. They will be priests of God and the Messiah and will rule with him. God will be among them, making his home with them, and there won't be any more death, grief, crying or pain.

John saw the thrones of the elect who were reigning with Christ for a thousand years (Rev 20:4–6). He saw the martyrs who had died during the Great Tribulation. Jesus had told the church at Laodicea, that he would enable those who conquer to share his throne, just as he had conquered and shared his Father's throne (Rev 3:21). The twenty-four elders sang a new song (Rev 5:9–10), saying that Jesus had been killed and with his blood had redeemed people for God *from every tribe, language, people and nation,* and that he had *made them a kingdom* and priests for God, and that *they would reign over the earth.* To make people a kingdom is to confer a kingdom upon them, to put them in positions of authority. The "kingdom" in this sense is the kingship or government of those who rule. The saints are children of God and everyone in God's household is a ruler.

Paul told Timothy, that if we endure, we will reign with Christ (2 Tim 2:12). Jesus promised his twelve apostles that in the new world, when he sits on his glorious throne, they would sit on thrones, judging the twelve tribes of Israel (Matt 19:28). Putting all this together, it is clear that all the righteous will rule with Christ during the millennium; not just those who are martyred during the Great Tribulation. This New Testament teaching is based on Daniel's prophecy that the kingdom and the dominion and the greatness of the kingdoms under the whole heaven would be given to the saints (Dan 7:27).

The saints will receive and possess the kingdom forever (Dan 7:18). Blessed are the poor in spirit, for theirs is the kingdom of heaven. Blessed are the meek, for they will inherit the earth. If we endure, we will reign with him (2 Tim 2:12). Blessed and holy are those who share in the first resurrection! They will reign with the Messiah for a thousand years (Rev 20:6).

The saints are the future rulers of the world. The Jews saw themselves as the saints in Daniel's prophecy, but progressive revelation shows that it is the church who will reign, including born-again Jews. In rejecting Jesus, the unbelieving Jews forfeited their right (Matt 21:43). The saints will have authority over the nations and will rule them with a rod of iron (Rev 2:26). They will be priests of God and of the Messiah. Our priesthood under the Messiah will be a mediatorial service that declares his will to the subjects of the kingdom. The saints will spread the knowledge of God to the nations, giving instructions on how they should live and obey and worship the King. And they will continually worship him themselves. The throne-room vision in Revelation 4 has twenty-five thrones; the throne of God is surrounded by twenty-four thrones on whom are seated twenty-four elders. Only humans are created in the image of God, and only humans are appointed by God to rule the world as his regents. These twenty-four elders are representatives of the elect, twelve representing the tribes of Israel, and twelve representing the apostles of the church. Cf. Rev 21:12–14 where the twelve gates of the New Jerusalem are named after the twelve tribes and the twelve foundations are named after the twelve apostles.

In addition to being appointed priests and rulers, the righteous will be rewarded according to their faithfulness and service for the Lord. In the parable of the ten coins, the nobleman commended the good and faithful servants and told one he would have authority over ten cities, and another that he would have authority over five cities (Lk19:11–27). Obedience in this life will result in greater responsibility and status in the millennium. In the chapter on the resurrection, Paul tells us to be steadfast, immovable, always abounding in the work of the Lord, knowing that in the Lord our labor is not in vain (1 Cor 15:58).

The world will be completely transformed. Eye hasn't seen, and ear hasn't heard, and man hasn't imagined what God has prepared for those who love him (1 Cor 2:9). It will be more beautiful and glorious and interesting than our wildest dreams. Wild animals will no longer be dangerous and agriculture will flourish. Among the subjects, there will be an ever-decreasing occurrence of war, crime, corruption, pain, mourning, tears and destructive weather.

The kingdom will be a theocracy. The population of the world will be ruled by the Messiah "with an iron rod". It will be a long era of peace, justice and righteousness (Isa 9:6). The earth will be filled with the knowledge of the Lord as the waters cover the sea (Isa 11:9). Instruction will go forth from Jerusalem and all nations will make pilgrimages there. The nations will beat their swords into plowshares; they'll manufacture tools instead of weaponry, and wars will cease worldwide (Isa 2:3–4). The subjects of the kingdom will live normal human lives farming, building houses and bearing children (Isa 65:21–23).

The King will reign from his throne in the New Jerusalem (Rev 22:3). As the Messiah, he will rule as the promised descendant of David as prophesied by the latter prophets (Isa 9:7, 11:1, Jer 23:5, 33:14–18, Ezek 34:23–24, Hos 3:5). Jerusalem itself will be raised up high and the surrounding area will be lowered as a plain (Isa 2:2, Zech 14:10–11).

The monarchy will be resurrected at Jesus' return. Those governing the world will have immortal, imperishable bodies (1 Cor 15:50–52). They will not live with the subjects; they will live in the New Jerusalem which will come down out of heaven from God (Rev 21:2–22:5). The description of the New Jerusalem is very symbolic, reflecting the beauty, perfection and glory of the home of the righteous. God himself is there with them and they will rule with him over the earth (Rev 5:9–10). The millennial Jerusalem and the New Jerusalem are intricately related, but they are not the same. The light of New Jerusalem will be seen above the earthly Jerusalem, but the community will exist in a different dimension.

During the millennium, the earth will be restored to its original condition as God created it. It is described as the new heavens and the new earth (Isa 65:17, 66:21–22, Rev 21:1, 2 Pet 3:13), but is better translated as 'the renewed sky and earth'. Jesus called it a 'new world', a 'regeneration' or 'the renewal of all things' (Matt 19:28). Peter, preaching in Jerusalem after the resurrection, said that heaven had received Christ until the time for restoring all things about which God had spoken by the mouth of his holy prophets long ago (Acts 3:21). Paul wrote that all creation waits with eager longing for the revealing of the sons of God, when the creation will be set free from its bondage to corruption and obtain the freedom of the glory of the children of God (Rom 8:19–21). The curse which was imposed on the earth's visible surface (Gen 3:17) will be progressively removed. During Messiah's reign, he will renew the earth until there are no more natural disasters. The wolf will live with the lamb, and the leopard with the young goat (Isa 11:6–9). What better way to describe the harmony of a perfected earth? What is said about the animal world will also be true about all God's creatures, including harmful bacteria and viruses. The world will return to the perfection of Eden. This regeneration will start with the nation of Israel and from there spread out over all the earth (Isa 51:4–5). The Messiah's resting place will be glorious. Isaiah speaks of the future glory of Jerusalem (Isa 60) and some of the verses are quoted to describe the New Jerusalem (Rev 21:23–25). All the nations will help with the rebuilding of Jerusalem. The last enemy, death, will finally be destroyed at the end of the millennium.

The devastation during the Great Tribulation will be enormous, as described by Isaiah 24. The Lord will empty the earth and make it desolate; he will twist its surface and scatter its inhabitants. They will be scorched, and few people will be left. The cities will lie in ruins.

The earth will be utterly broken, split apart, and violently shaken (Isa 24:1–19).

When the angel pours out the last bowl of God's wrath, there will be a great earthquake, such as has never occurred since man has been on the earth, and the cities will collapse (Rev 16:17–19). The sun and moon will become be darkened, mountains will crumble, and islands will be submerged (Rev 6:12, 14).

So, the Lord's first task will be to restore the desolated earth. Civilization will start again from scratch. In John's one verse description of the new earth, he said that the sea was no more. That doesn't mean the world will have any less water, but its distribution would be different; more lakes and rivers, more subterranean water or a greater cloud covering.

However, there is another, more likely, interpretation. Zechariah sad that the Messiah's rule will extend from sea to sea (Zech 9:10), and "on that day" living waters will flow out from Jerusalem, half of them to the Dead Sea and half of them to the Mediterranean (Zech 14:8–9). The word "sea" is often used metaphorically in the Bible for the rebellious and turbulent nations. David says that God stills the roaring of the seas, the roaring of their waves, and the turmoil of the nations (Ps 65:7). Psalm 89:9 says that God rules over the surging sea; when its waves mount up, he stills them. Isaiah 17:12 says:

Oh, the raging of many nations, they rage like the raging sea! Oh, the uproar of the peoples – they roar like the roaring of great waters!

When Daniel had a vision of the world's great kingdoms, he saw four great beasts coming out of the sea (Dan 7:2–3, 17), and John saw Satan standing on the shore of the sea just before he saw the final world empire emerging from the sea (Rev 13:1). In these verses one can see that "sea" is often used as a metaphor for the turbulent sinful nations. When John says that the sea was no more (Rev 21:1), he is more than likely using the word symbolically, meaning that the new world will be at peace, without the turbulence created by warring nations.

Large cities, especially megacities will no longer be on the agenda. We can't be sure what technology will be deemed beneficial, or what transport or education, but the world will be freed from the tragic effects of sin and the curse. Everything will be recreated. The future hope that many Christians through the ages have always vaguely thought about as "heaven" will actually be a renewed earth. The redeemed saints will be totally fulfilled in their role as rulers and teachers and managers of the new world.

At the end of the thousand years, Satan will be released from his prison in the abyss, and he will go out once again to test the faithfulness of mankind. He is the spirit who works in those who are disobedient (Eph 2:2) and he will soon succeed in instigating a rebellion. Despite the thousand years of peace and righteousness and submission to God, humanity will once again be deceived and will march defiantly from all directions towards Jerusalem, the camp of God's people. The word "camp" alludes to the Israel camp in the wilderness that was a ceremonially clean area around the tabernacle where the Israelites had their tents (Num 5:1–4). Satan's armies will go and surround the earthly Jerusalem, not the New Jerusalem and the resurrected saints. Fire will come down from heaven and consume them and the devil will be captured and thrown into hell (Rev 20:9–10). The last resurrection and judgment will follow (Rev 20:12–13.).

The millennial city of Jerusalem and its temple will be a glorious place and in need of the world's resources. All nations will go there to worship, and the kings of the earth will bring their splendor into it (Isa 60:9–11, Hag 2:7–9, Rev 21:24).

Only the redeemed can enter the New Jerusalem, so the nations and kings can't bring their wealth there, it would be superfluous. These nations are the unregenerate survivors of the nations, but they will be healed of their animosities through God's word that goes forth from Zion.

When John saw his vision of the future Jerusalem, he saw the glorified New Jerusalem, but in Revelation 21:24–25 he saw its earthly counterpart, described by the Old Testament prophets as an exalted city in the land of Israel, raised upon a mountain above a vast plain. The nations come to its light, the kings bring their wealth into it and its gates are never shut. The earthly Jerusalem is inhabited by God's chosen people, the Jews, and the world is characterized by peace and righteousness and the knowledge of the Lord as the Messiah reigns. The nations of the world are the unbelievers who survived the Great Tribulation and now live in submission to the King of kings. They bring their worldly resources to Jerusalem and give honor to the king. Nearly all of the latter prophets talk about a glorified Jerusalem, with Israel victorious, and their former enemies living peacefully, but in submission to them.

These two cities are one, but in different dimensions. Paul speaks of the present Jerusalem and of the Jerusalem above (Gal 4:25–26), which Hebrews 12:22 calls the heavenly Jerusalem. The New Jerusalem will come down out of heaven in close proximity to the earth. The saints will share the Messiah's throne (kingship), the earthly throne of David, not the eternal throne of God (Rev 3:21).

The New Jerusalem is the abode of the redeemed, those whose names are written in the Lamb's book of life and who will reign with the Messiah. They don't marry or have babies (Matt 22:30). The apostles were promised that they would rule over Israel, so other saints may likewise rule over areas where they lived and served God previously. They will be a kingdom of priests who serve as mediators between God and the world's population.

There is a river whose streams make glad the city of God, the holy place where the Most High dwells (Ps 46:4). The river that Ezekiel saw flowing from the south side of the temple in Jerusalem (Ezek 47) flows into the Dead Sea and makes its salt water become fresh. Zechariah says that living water will flow out of Jerusalem, half to the eastern sea, which is the Dead Sea, and half to the western sea which is the Mediterranean (Zech 14:8). This river is a symbolic representation of the regeneration, not only of Palestine, but of the entire world, a renewal that the Messiah will bring about as he rules the world in righteousness and justice and peace.

16. THE MESSIAH'S THRONE

The angel Gabriel told Mary that God would give her child *the throne of his father David* and he would reign over the house of Jacob forever. His kingdom would never end (Luke 1:32–33). Even though Mary was probably a teenager, she would have understood these words as a promise that God would make her son Jesus king over Israel. He would give him the kingship and he would reign in Jerusalem. The most satisfactory interpretation of Gabriel's statement for us is that after his return, Jesus the Messiah will reign over Israel during the millennium. If not then, when will he reign over Israel?

Jesus promised his disciples that when he sits on his glorious throne in the new world, they would sit on twelve thrones judging the twelve tribes of Israel (Matt 19:28). The new world is a rebirth or a regeneration of the world when the Messiah returns. The saints will reign with him over the survivors of the Great Tribulation, the final seven years of this world's troubled history. The apostles will rule over a newly converted Israel, while other overcomers will rule elsewhere in the world. Jesus will give us the right to share his throne (reign) and rule with him during the millennium, just as he shares his Father's throne and rules with him.

The New Testament emphasizes the fact that at the ascension, Jesus sat down at the right hand of God, where he is sharing God the Father's throne. The significance of this is that a man, Jesus, with a glorified, resurrected, human body, is now on the throne with his Father; humanity exalted to deity. In reality God the Son never left his throne. Jesus told his disciples that he never did anything on his own initiative; he only did what he saw the Father doing. He even made the bold statement that whatever the Father does, he, the Son, also does. He is God and he reigns forever. Three times in John, Jesus uses the phrase "where I am" to inform his disciples that even though he was with them in the world, he was still with the Father (John 12:26, 14:3, 17:24). Jesus was always very conscious of the fact that he was one with the Father and of the glory that he had with him before the world began.

Another important throne passage is Matthew 25:31 ff. which says that when the Messiah returns in his glory and all the angels are with him, he will sit on his glorious throne, from where he will judge the nations. The righteous will inherit the kingdom prepared for them from the foundation of the world, while the unrighteous will be consigned to the eternal fire prepared for the devil and his angels. The separation of the sheep from the goats symbolizes the fact that all mankind will be separated into two groups, the righteous and the wicked.

The background to these verses is found in several Psalms which elaborate on God's promise to David in 2 Samuel 7:16 to establish *his throne* forever. In Psalm 2, God declares that he will set his regent on Zion, his holy hill. He will give him the nations as his inheritance and the ends of the earth as his possession. He will make him the highest of the kings of the earth and *his throne* will endure forever (Ps 89:27–29). The Lord will extend the Messiah's mighty scepter from Zion (Ps 110:2).

Peter, preaching on the day of Pentecost, said that David was a prophet and he knew that God had promised him on oath that he would put one of his descendants on *his throne*; Jesus, the promised Messiah.

Isaiah prophesied to his fellow Jews that a child would be born to them, a son given to them, and the government would be upon his shoulder. Of the increase of his government and of peace there would be no end. He would reign on *David's throne and over his kingdom*, establishing it and upholding it forever (Isa 9:6–7). In a vision, Daniel saw the Ancient of Days giving the Son of Man *dominion and glory and a kingdom*, so that all peoples, nations, and languages should serve him (Dan 7:14). The fulfillment of this came after his ascension, when Jesus told his disciples that *all authority in heaven and on earth* had been given to him (Mat 28:18). They should go and make disciples of all nations, because he is coming back to reign. If not on earth, where else are all nations, peoples and languages going to serve him

John, in his vision (Rev 20:5–6), saw the saints rising from the dead and reigning with the Messiah on earth (Rev 5:10) for a thousand years.

In Ezekiel's opening vision he saw the Lord and his glory accompanied by the cherubim; the same living creatures that John describes in Revelation 4. Later Ezekiel describes the glory of the Lord leaving *the temple* in Jerusalem via the east gate and the Mount of Olives because of Israel's sin (Ezek 11:23). Finally, Ezekiel sees the glory of the Lord returning to Jerusalem from the east (Ezek 43:1–9). The sound of his coming was like the roar of many waters, and the earth shone with the brilliance of his glory. The glory of the Lord entered *the temple* by the gate facing east and filled *the temple*. The glory of the Lord is equivalent to his presence. Ezekiel heard the Lord's voice speaking from *the temple* and telling him that this was the place of *his throne* and the place of the soles of his feet, where he would dwell among Israel forever (Ezek 43:7).

Ezekiel's vision of the return of the glory of the Lord to Jerusalem is nothing else but the return of the Lord Jesus Christ. Zechariah tells us that on that day his feet shall stand on the Mount of Olives that lies east of Jerusalem (Zech 14:4). The eastern gate to Jerusalem, facing the Mount of Olives, allows direct access to the temple. It was sealed by the Ottoman Sultan Suleiman in 1541, and Jewish tradition believes that when the Messiah returns, he will enter Jerusalem via this gate.

The prophet Malachi confirms that the Lord will suddenly come to *his temple*. He asks who will be able to endure the day of his coming, and who can stand when he appears? (Mal 3:1–2). These verses clarify somewhat the events surrounding Jesus' return as the Messiah. He will reign on earth from the temple in Jerusalem during the millennium.

This physical reign with Christ on planet earth should not be confused with our spiritual exaltation. God has already raised us up with Christ and seated us with him in heaven. Being seated with Christ spiritually on God's throne is our present status (Eph 1:20, 2:6). It is in anticipation of our ruling physically with him on his own glorious throne over the earth (Rev 5:10).

For how long will Jesus reign? Can his kingdom go on forever and ever, for eternity? Gabriel told Mary that Jesus will reign over Israel *forever*, and that his kingdom will *have no end* (Luke 1:33). Daniel mentions many times that the Messiah's kingdom is everlasting and will never be destroyed (Dan 2:44, 7:14, 27). And those who are wise will shine like the stars forever and ever. Paul tells of the Son handing the kingdom (kingship or reign) over to the Father (1 Cor 15:24). This will happen on judgment day, after the millennium, when we are told that earth and sky will flee from God's presence and no place will be found for them. As that signals the end of the world, the Messiah's visible kingdom and his kingship will pass from Son to Father, so that the Father might have full authority over everything. However, the Son and the saints will continue to rule with him, because they have been promised eternal rule.

There are several scriptures that indicate that the earth will perish, wear out like a garment, and pass away (Ps 102:25, cf. Heb 1:11–12). Jesus made the statement that heaven and earth will pass away, but his words will not pass away (Matt 24:35). The creation is not eternal. In Hebrews 12:27 we are told that we will receive a kingdom that cannot be shaken. The sky and earth will wear out like a garment, God will roll them up like a robe, and like a garment they will be changed.

But, is this annihilation or transformation? Hebrews 12:26–27 prophesies the removal of things that can be shaken, so that the things that cannot be shaken may remain. It is a quote from Haggai 2:6–7 where it says that God will shake all nations so that their treasures might fill the (millennial) temple with glory. Haggai is not talking about an annihilation. His shaking of the heavens and the earth and the sea and the dry land are to do with the Great Tribulation and the complete transformation which will take place in the world when the kingdom of the world becomes the kingdom of the Lord and his Messiah. Isaiah also prophesies that the wealth of the nations will be brought to Jerusalem (Isa 60:5) and John confirms it in his vision (Rev 21:24–26).

There is no promise of a new physical creation, but the presence of the four living creatures around God's throne indicates that the animal kingdom will continue to exist, at least during the millennium. The redeemed will continue their existence in what is called the New Jerusalem, where there is no sun or night, and where they will reign forever (Rev 22:5). Paul spoke about God's wisdom which he decreed before time began for our glory. He said nobody has seen or heard or imagined what it will be like (1 Cor 2:9), so theologians, philosophers and scientists can be assured that the future will be bright for the redeemed. Nobody knows the details.

17. The Saints will Rule the World

The meek will inherit the earth, Jesus said. That is a statement that cannot be spiritualized, as some people do with passages that concern the Messiah's reign over the earth with his saints. The Bible does not teach that the Messiah, or the saints, are ruling on earth now. They will reign over the earth in the future. Paul told the Corinthian Christians that the saints would judge (rule) the world (1 Cor 6:2). At the Last Supper, Jesus conferred on his disciples a kingdom, just as his Father had conferred one on him, so that they might eat and drink at his table in his kingdom and sit on thrones, judging the twelve tribes of Israel (Luke 22:29–30). This suggests a banquet at the king's palace during the messianic reign.

The reign of the saints over the world, as taught in the New Testament, is firmly based on the predictions of the prophet Daniel, who clearly stated that the saints of the Most High would receive the kingdom and possess it forever (Dan 7:18). Then he repeated that the kingdom and the dominion and the greatness of the kingdoms under the whole heaven would be given to the people of the saints of the Most High (Dan 7:27). On the basis of this prophecy, Jesus pronounced his benedictions on the poor in spirit, the meek and those who are persecuted for righteousness' sake, saying that they would inherit the earth, because the kingdom of heaven is theirs (Matt 5:3, 5, 10).

Nevertheless, there is mystery about the future reign of Christ. We are not given a clear picture of how he will rule the world during those thousand years. We know what he will accomplish, and we know that the saints will reign with him. Is it not possible to conclude that the Messiah and the saints will frequent two different dimensions during the millennium, just as Jesus did after his resurrection?

The elect will live in the presence of God and the Messiah. There will be no more death or tears or pain, and they will be fully satisfied. Their status will be that of God's sons, princes, and they will reign with

God and the Messiah forever. This future life, which John describes in Revelation 21:2 – 22:5, begins at the resurrection, at the moment when the elect become supernatural beings. Their reign over the earth will continue for the duration of the millennium. In the resurrection the saints will be like angels, their existence will be in another dimension, but being "in Christ" they will participate in the millennial kingdom. They will inherit the kingdom, and as the monarchy, they will rule over the earth (Rev 5:10). The New Jerusalem has twelve gates with the names of the tribes of Israel and twelve foundations with the names of the apostles. All the elect from Israel and the church will be included, all whose names are written in the Lamb's book of life.

Jesus' experience after his resurrection may be the best guide to understanding their existence in the world to come. He appeared to his disciples over a period of forty days but disappeared at will to another dimension. While in the world with his disciples he was fully human: he spoke with them, he breathed on them, he ate with them. He showed them his body and they touched him. He said that he wasn't a ghost but had flesh and bones. On several occasions, he appeared to people and they didn't recognize him, or weren't sure. For example: Mary Magdalene at the tomb, the disciples on the Emmaus road, the disciples while fishing, and when Jesus was with the eleven in Galilee. He had miraculous powers; he walked through walls, and he produced a fire of burning coals, with fish on it and some bread. While serving the Messiah as a kingdom of priests, during the millennium, the saints' existence may be like that of Jesus, appearing to people as normal humans, but not living among them. The teaching that we will meet the Lord in the air at the resurrection assumes that we will have the ability to travel through space.

Zechariah 9:9 is messianic and describes Jesus' triumphant entry into Jerusalem. He told them that their king was coming to them, righteous and having salvation, gentle and riding on a colt, the foal of a donkey. Then in verse 10 he jumps over to the millennial reign, saying that the Messiah will proclaim peace to the nations, his rule will extend from sea to sea, and from the Euphrates River to the ends of the earth. The last sentence is from Psalm 72:8 which anticipates a worldwide rule of the Messiah. These texts should not be spiritualized, when a literal interpretation is so well supported by other scriptures.

Jesus told his apostles that when he sits on his glorious throne in the renewed creation, they would also sit on twelve thrones, governing the twelve tribes of Israel (Matt 19:28). The whole church will rule with the Messiah over the survivors of the Great Tribulation.

18. The Last Judgment

Satan will be released after the millennial reign and he will foment a final rebellion against Jerusalem. Fire will come down from heaven and devour them and Satan will be cast into hell (Rev 20:7–10). The judge in Revelation 20:11–15 is not named, but "he who is seated on the throne" is universally thought of as God, but we wouldn't be wrong if we interpreted the judge to be Jesus the Messiah. Jesus made it very clear that the Father judges no one, he has given all judgment to the Son (John 5:22). The one seated on the throne is God, whether Father or Son.

The context is the very end of this world. John said that the earth and sky will flee from God's presence and no place will be found for them (Rev 20:11). What has been made and is transitory will be removed, so that only what is eternal will remain (Heb 12:27). That sounds like the end of the physical creation, the world and maybe the entire universe.

This is followed by the final judgment of the wicked and their consignment to hell (Rev 20:12–15). Everyone will be judged according to what he/she has done. Anyone whose name is not found written in the book of life will be thrown into hell. The end of the physical creation is expressed succinctly in Revelation 20:11, where earth and sky flee from God's presence, and no place is found for them. Compare Hebrews 12:26–29.

When the judgment is over, death and Hades and anyone whose name is not found in the book of life will be thrown into the lake of fire which is a metaphor for hell. The Antichrist, the false prophet and the devil were previously consigned to this fate and will be tormented there forever. Death being thrown into a lake of fire can only mean one thing; its annihilation. The same goes for Hades, the realm of the dead. In Matthew's Gospel Jesus described hell six times as a place of wailing and the gnashing of teeth for evil people.

The Last Judgment is mainly for the damned as most of the righteous will have been reigning with the Messiah for a thousand years. But millennial converts, including Israel, will be resurrected, judged and found righteous. There is no condemnation for those who are in union with the Messiah Jesus (Rom 8:1).

The judgment seat of Christ (1 Cor 3:13, 2 Cor 5:10) is for all believers and can be compared to passing through a fire. The true value of all their attitudes and deeds will be made manifest and individuals will be rewarded accordingly. There is no punishment for sins, that is covered by the blood of Christ, but rewards may be withheld, and some will suffer loss, because it will be a divine assessment of their worth. This judgment will occur at or soon after the resurrection, so that rewards might be enjoyed during that millennium.

In the parable about the 'sheep' and the 'goats' (Matt 25), the righteous and wicked are all judged at the same time. It is a parable, as are the other passages in that chapter, and the details should not be taken too literally. The judgment of the righteous takes place before the millennium, because they are invited to inherit the kingdom prepared for them from the foundation of the world. The emphasis of this parable is not on the timing of the judgment, but on the basis of judgment, which is the attitude people have toward the Messiah's brethren. Their faith is shown by what they did during their lifetimes to help fellow Christians.

Following the last judgment, the Messiah will surrender his kingship to God the Father, because his role as ruler is an earthly role and it has now come to an end (1 Cor 15:24).

19. SATAN

In Job 1:6 Satan is numbered among the sons of God who are defined as those who were around when God laid the foundation of the earth (Job 38:4, 7). Maybe the words of Ezekiel 28:15–17 apply to him: "You were blameless in your behavior from the day you were created until wickedness was discovered in you. ... Your heart grew arrogant because of your beauty; you annihilated your own wisdom because of your splendor."

Father and Son rule the universe, but the planet earth is under the control of this power that John calls the evil one (1 John 5:19) and Paul calls Satan. Paul says he is the ruler of the power of the air, the spirit that is active in those who are disobedient (Eph 2:2). He warns Christians that their real struggle is not against human opponents, but against rulers, authorities, cosmic powers in the darkness around us, and evil spiritual forces in the heavenly realm (Eph 6:12). The heavenly realm here has the same meaning as "air" in Ephesians 2:2. Satan is the ruler of the power of the air. The evil spiritual forces Paul is talking about are evil spirits or demons. This teaching should not be considered an anachronism; the presence of evil spirits is very evident in many parts of the world.

From his heavenly throne Jesus poured out the Holy Spirit at Pentecost, and in heaven he intercedes with the Father for the saints. All powers in heaven are in submission to Jesus (1 Pet 3:22), he is superior to them all, but he won't rule the world until he returns as the conquering Messiah. Meanwhile he is waiting for the day when his enemies will be made a footstool for his feet (Heb 10:13). God will subdue the enemies at the climax of the Great Tribulation when Jesus returns. The major defeat will be at Armageddon, when God destroys the Antichrist and his evil empire. It is only after that event that the Messiah will begin his rule and he will reign until he puts all remaining enemies under his feet (1 Cor 15:25).

At the Messiah's return, Satan will be captured and incarcerated in the Abyss (Rev 20:1–3). The prophet Isaiah predicted this event and the millennial reign that follows (Isa 24:21–22). He said that the Lord would punish the armies of the exalted ones above, and the rulers of the earth on earth. They will be herded together into the Pit, shut up in prison, and *after many days* they will be punished. The armies opposing the Lord at Armageddon will be defeated, whether spiritual or human, and the evil spirits and the souls of the human opponents will be thrown together into the bottomless pit. These are the angels that have been cast into the lowest hell, chained in darkness until judgment day (2 Pet 2:4, Jude 6). From that time on the Messiah and his fellow victors will be enthroned in glory on Mount Zion (Rev 14:1).

According to God's plan, when the thousand years are over, Satan will be released from his prison and will again incite the nations into rebelling against God and his people. They will march from all over the earth to Jerusalem, but they will suddenly be destroyed by fire from heaven and Satan will be cast into hell to be tormented forever (Rev 20:7–10). This will spell the end of the forces of evil that have plagued mankind from the time that Adam and Eve were deceived by the serpent's cunning in the garden of Eden. That this final battle is different to Armageddon is shown by the fact that the Antichrist and the false prophet were thrown into hell immediately after Armageddon (Rev 19:20), while now, after the millennium, Satan is thrown into hell where the beast and the false prophet had previously been thrown (Rev 20:10).

The Bible blames Satan for the origin of sin and suffering in the world. It was he who, in the form of a snake, tempted Adam and Eve. They disobeyed God and were driven out of the garden. However, his doom was immediately pronounced by God when he declared that the offspring of the woman (the Messiah) would crush his head (Gen 3:15). In the book of Job, we see why Satan is called the "accuser of the brethren". He accused Job of insincerity in his worship of God, but was proved wrong. In the Gospels, a large part of Jesus' ministry consisted of exorcisms and the healing of people who were afflicted by the devil. The apostle John declared that the whole world lies under the control of the evil one (1 John 5:19). The apostle Paul told the Ephesian Christians that they once lived according to the ways of this present world and according to the ruler of the power of the air, the spirit that is now active in those who are disobedient (Eph 2:1–2).

His existence, and that of demons and evil spirits throughout the world is very real. Westerners may doubt his existence, because in the West his activities have become more sophisticated, but in some countries like Italy and Ireland, requests for exorcisms are on the increase and in 2018 the Vatican held a training course for exorcists. Throughout Africa, India and in South American countries where voodoo is rife, the existence of evil supernatural forces is not in doubt. It is clearly evidenced by the prevalence of demon possession and the effectiveness of black magic. Possessed people covet the sense of power the possessing spirit gives them. Some exhibit supernatural strength, others speak in ancient languages they have never learnt. Jesus called Satan "the ruler of this world" three times in John's Gospel (John 12:31, 14:30, 16:11).

If the devil has this enormous power and authority, how does that relate to the kingdom of God? When Jesus was tempted by the devil before he began his ministry, it was in regard to kingdom authority. The devil took him to a high place and showed him *all the kingdoms of the world* in an instant. Then he told Jesus he would give him all that authority, because it had been given to him to give to whoever he wanted. If only Jesus would worship him, all that glory would be his (Luke 4:5–7). Jesus rejected the offer because the Father had his own plan and way of giving him the kingdom.

During the last week before the crucifixion, Jesus said it was now time for the judgment of this world to begin. *The ruler of this world will be thrown out* (John 12:31). Jesus' triumph over Satan at the cross was decisive, but not immediate. As we have seen above, the apostles still regarded Satan as being very active in the world. He has suffered a fatal blow, but from where has he been cast out? Certainly not from the world. Jesus told the seventy-two disciples whom he sent out to preach and heal that he saw Satan fall like lightning from *heaven* (Luke 10:18). Jesus disabled the rulers and the authorities, he made a public spectacle of them, triumphing over them in the cross (Col 2:15). Because of his death he will destroy the devil who has the power of death (Heb 2:14), but the devil is still prowling around looking for someone to devour (1 Pet 5:8), and we still need to resist him.

It is not until Revelation 12:9 that we read that Satan and his angels will be defeated by Michael and his angels and thrown down to the earth. His time on earth will be short, the last three and a half years of the Great Tribulation (Rev 12:12–14). He will come down in great anger, intent on destroying God's plan for Israel and the church and preventing the messianic kingdom from taking place. But, the martyrs at that time will conquer Satan by their reliance on the blood of the Lamb and by the confession of their faith. They will not cling to their lives even in the face of death (Rev 12:11).

Satan and his cohorts are judicially defeated but obviously still very active in the world, trying to thwart God's purposes. That is something to remember when we, as God's children, are being tempted or persecuted. There is no evidence that the activities of these evil forces have changed since the crucifixion. Satan is still as active as he ever was, he is not yet bound.

G. Eldon Ladd (A Commentary on the Revelation of John p. 173) says that the martyrdom of the martyrs is their victory over Satan. It is proof that his accusations against them are empty. They follow in the steps of their master. Since God's children are made of flesh and blood, God the Son also took on flesh and blood, so that by his death he might destroy the devil who had the power of death, and that he might free those who were in slavery during their lives to the fear of death (Heb 2:14–15).

The Messiah's death on the cross has far-reaching benefits. Through Jesus' shed blood on the cross, God reconciled all things to himself, making peace with things on earth and things in heaven (Col 1:20). Jesus' death on the cross has made possible a reconciliation between God and creation. Because of Jesus' redemptive work on the cross, he will be able to set creation free from its bondage to decay during the millennium. In addition, those who are redeemed and empowered by the Holy Spirit have the ability to overcome sin and evil forces. Christians are far less likely than unbelievers to be possessed by evil spirits or be affected by black magic. Even Muslims seek refuge from these evil powers in church communities. The devil has been bound to some degree as far as the righteous are concerned, but he is still ruling over the world of unbelievers. He will continue to do evil, sow tares, and hinder Christian workers, until the Messiah comes. Then he will be put out of action and cast into the Abyss for a thousand years.

His last strategy will be to empower the last world empire and ultimately, the Antichrist. He will not only give him great power and authority over every tribe, people, language, and nation, but also his kingship (Rev 13:2b). This final world dictator will be the most powerful and evil dictator that the world has ever known. The ensuing persecution and defeat of the saints will be the final suffering the church will endure before Christ's return, and it will be extensive; there will be many martyrs all over the world in those last days. Christians are called on not only to be believe in Christ, but also to suffer for him.

20. Signs of Jesus' Return

Evangelization of the World
Worldwide Rebellion
Globalization
Return of Israel to the World Stage

Signs that the Messiah is coming soon are increasing: First, there is worldwide evangelization. Jesus said the gospel of the kingdom would be proclaimed throughout the whole world as a testimony to all nations, and then the end will come (Matt 24:14). Note that it is the gospel of the kingdom that will be proclaimed. The good news of the cross could not be understood by his disciples at that time, for them it was the kingdom they longed for. The good news in Matthew is always to do with the coming of the messianic kingdom, or by metonymy, the coming of the Messiah.

A rebellion will occur before Jesus returns, a worldwide rejection of God, his word, his church and his people Israel, resulting from an embrace of humanism. This is the spirit of antichrist. With the loss of godly and quality political leadership, civilization will collapse. Then the lawless one, the man of sin, also called the Antichrist, will arise and exalt himself over everything that is called God or is worshiped. He will eventually set himself up in God's temple in Jerusalem, the final center of resistance, proclaiming himself to be God (2 Thess 2:3–4). His aim will be to have a godless society, except for himself. He is presently being held back by a "restrainer", in my mind, the Bible. Once the Bible is banned worldwide, then the lawless one will be revealed. In Satan's power, he will perform miracles, signs and wonders, and deceive those who are now living in spiritual darkness.

The Antichrist's rise to power will be preceded by increasing globalization and a world-wide empire. After persecuting the church for three and a half years, during which time a great multitude of believers will be martyred (Rev 7:9, 14), he will be overthrown by the Lord Jesus at his coming.

The return of Israel to their land was prophesied by many of the Jewish prophets. About 6.5 million Jews (2018) are now living in Israel. The apostle Paul makes it clear that God has *not* finished with Israel. God's gifts and his call are irrevocable (Rom 11:29). There are many prophecies that Israel as a nation will be converted in the last days (Isa 59:20–21, Jer 31:33–34, Joel 3:16–17, Zech 8:7–8, 12:10). They will become believers in Jesus *after* the Messiah returns and defeats their enemies who will, at that time, have surrounded Jerusalem.

The Messiah will then rule over his people Israel from their capital city of Jerusalem, ruling the whole world as King of kings and Lord of lords, reigning over all the survivors of the Great Tribulation.

I don't think that we should ignore the fact that the church is nearly two-thousand years old. The church began at Pentecost, fifty days after the Passover in the year that Jesus was crucified. Some scholars think that he died in AD 30 when he would have been thirty-three years old, others think he died in AD 33 when he would have been thirty six. There is sure to be much speculation about Jesus returning on the church's two-thousandth anniversary or thereabouts, around 2030 to 2033. If that were to be the case, the Great Tribulation would have to begin in a very short time.

Jesus is coming soon. Be ready!

21. The Seven Benedictions of Revelation

1. Those who read John's book are blessed, and more to the point, those who pay attention to what is written in it (Rev 1:3).

2. Those who endure and die in the Lord in times of persecution (14.12–13).

3. Those who remain vigilant and prepared and are not deceived by Satan's propaganda. Others will be caught out naked and ashamed (16:15).

4. Those who are invited to the wedding supper of the Lamb! (19:9).

5. Those who have part in the first resurrection. They won't be thrown into hell; they will be priests of God and of Christ and will reign with him for a thousand years (20:6).

6. Those who keeps the words of the prophecy in this book, those who stand fast and endure to the end (22:7).

7. Those who wash their robes and keep them clean by not compromising with the Antichrist's demands. They will have the right to the tree of life and will have free access into the holy city (22:14).

Lightning Source UK Ltd.
Milton Keynes UK
UKHW040718050320
359822UK00001B/201